Building an Electronic Records Archive at the National Archives and Records Administration

Recommendations for Initial Development

Committee on Digital Archiving
and the National Archives and Records Administration

Computer Science and Telecommunications Board

NATIONAL RESEARCH COUNCIL
OF THE NATIONAL ACADEMIES

Robert F. Sproull and Jon Eisenberg, Editors

THE NATIONAL ACADEMIES PRESS
Washington, D.C.
www.nap.edu

THE NATIONAL ACADEMIES PRESS   500 Fifth Street, N.W.   Washington, DC 20001

NOTICE: The project that is the subject of this report was approved by the Governing Board of the National Research Council, whose members are drawn from the councils of the National Academy of Sciences, the National Academy of Engineering, and the Institute of Medicine. The members of the committee responsible for the report were chosen for their special competences and with regard for appropriate balance.

Support for this project was provided by the National Archives and Records Administration under Contract No. NAMA-02-C-0012. Any opinions, findings, conclusions, or recommendations expressed in this publication are those of the authors and do not necessarily reflect the views of the organizations that provided support for the project.

International Standard Book Number 0-309-08947-6 (Book)
International Standard Book Number 0-309-51729-X (PDF)

Copies of this report are available from the National Academies Press, 500 Fifth Street, N.W., Lockbox 285, Washington, DC 20055. Telephone (800) 624-6242 or (202) 334-3313 in the Washington metropolitan area. Internet, http://www.nap.edu.

Copyright 2003 by the National Academy of Sciences. All rights reserved.

Printed in the United States of America

THE NATIONAL ACADEMIES
Advisers to the Nation on Science, Engineering, and Medicine

The **National Academy of Sciences** is a private, nonprofit, self-perpetuating society of distinguished scholars engaged in scientific and engineering research, dedicated to the furtherance of science and technology and to their use for the general welfare. Upon the authority of the charter granted to it by the Congress in 1863, the Academy has a mandate that requires it to advise the federal government on scientific and technical matters. Dr. Bruce M. Alberts is president of the National Academy of Sciences.

The **National Academy of Engineering** was established in 1964, under the charter of the National Academy of Sciences, as a parallel organization of outstanding engineers. It is autonomous in its administration and in the selection of its members, sharing with the National Academy of Sciences the responsibility for advising the federal government. The National Academy of Engineering also sponsors engineering programs aimed at meeting national needs, encourages education and research, and recognizes the superior achievements of engineers. Dr. Wm. A. Wulf is president of the National Academy of Engineering.

The **Institute of Medicine** was established in 1970 by the National Academy of Sciences to secure the services of eminent members of appropriate professions in the examination of policy matters pertaining to the health of the public. The Institute acts under the responsibility given to the National Academy of Sciences by its congressional charter to be an adviser to the federal government and, upon its own initiative, to identify issues of medical care, research, and education. Dr. Harvey V. Fineberg is president of the Institute of Medicine.

The **National Research Council** was organized by the National Academy of Sciences in 1916 to associate the broad community of science and technology with the Academy's purposes of furthering knowledge and advising the federal government. Functioning in accordance with general policies determined by the Academy, the Council has become the principal operating agency of both the National Academy of Sciences and the National Academy of Engineering in providing services to the government, the public, and the scientific and engineering communities. The Council is administered jointly by both Academies and the Institute of Medicine. Dr. Bruce M. Alberts and Dr. Wm. A. Wulf are chair and vice chair, respectively, of the National Research Council.

www.national-academies.org

COMMITTEE ON DIGITAL ARCHIVING AND THE NATIONAL ARCHIVES AND RECORDS ADMINISTRATION

ROBERT F. SPROULL, Sun Microsystems, *Chair*
HOWARD BESSER, University of California, Los Angeles
JAMIE CALLAN, Carnegie Mellon University
CHARLES DOLLAR, Dollar Consulting
STUART HABER, Hewlett-Packard Laboratories
MARGARET HEDSTROM, University of Michigan
MARK KORNBLUH, Michigan State University
RAYMOND LORIE, IBM Almaden Research Center
CLIFFORD LYNCH, Coalition for Networked Information
JEROME H. SALTZER, Massachusetts Institute of Technology
MARGO SELTZER, Harvard University
ROBERT WILENSKY, University of California, Berkeley

Staff

JON EISENBERG, Study Director and Senior Program Officer
STEVEN WOO, Program Officer
DAVID PADGHAM, Research Associate
JENNIFER M. BISHOP, Senior Project Assistant

COMPUTER SCIENCE AND TELECOMMUNICATIONS BOARD

DAVID D. CLARK, Massachusetts Institute of Technology, *Chair*
ERIC BENHAMOU, 3Com Corporation
DAVID BORTH, Motorola Labs
JOHN M. CIOFFI, Stanford University
ELAINE COHEN, University of Utah
W. BRUCE CROFT, University of Massachusetts at Amherst
THOMAS E. DARCIE, University of Victoria
JOSEPH FARRELL, University of California at Berkeley
JOAN FEIGENBAUM, Yale University
HECTOR GARCIA MOLINA, Stanford University
WENDY KELLOGG, IBM Thomas J. Watson Research Center
BUTLER W. LAMPSON, Microsoft Corporation
DAVID LIDDLE, U.S. Venture Partners
TOM M. MITCHELL, Carnegie Mellon University
DAVID A. PATTERSON, University of California at Berkeley
HENRY (HANK) PERRITT, Chicago-Kent College of Law
DANIEL PIKE, GCI Cable and Entertainment
ERIC SCHMIDT, Google, Inc.
FRED SCHNEIDER, Cornell University
BURTON SMITH, Cray Inc.
LEE SPROULL, New York University
WILLIAM STEAD, Vanderbilt University
JEANNETTE M. WING, Carnegie Mellon University

MARJORY S. BLUMENTHAL, Director
KRISTEN BATCH, Research Associate
JENNIFER M. BISHOP, Senior Project Assistant
JANET BRISCOE, Administrative Officer
DAVID DRAKE, Senior Project Assistant
JON EISENBERG, Senior Program Officer
RENEE HAWKINS, Financial Associate
PHIL HILLIARD, Research Associate
MARGARET MARSH HUYNH, Senior Project Assistant
ALAN S. INOUYE, Senior Program Officer
HERBERT S. LIN, Senior Scientist
LYNETTE I. MILLETT, Program Officer
DAVID PADGHAM, Research Associate
CYNTHIA A. PATTERSON, Program Officer
JANICE SABUDA, Senior Project Assistant
BRANDYE WILLIAMS, Staff Assistant
STEVEN WOO, Dissemination Officer

For more information on CSTB, see its Web site at <http://www.cstb.org>, write to CSTB, National Research Council, 500 Fifth Street, N.W., Washington, DC 20001, call at (202) 334-2605, or e-mail the CSTB at cstb@nas.edu.

Preface

Like its constituent agencies and other organizations, the federal government generates and increasingly saves a large and growing fraction of its records in electronic form. Recognizing the greater and greater importance of these electronic records for its mission of preserving "essential evidence," the National Archives and Records Administration (NARA) launched a major new initiative, the Electronic Records Archives (ERA). NARA plans to commence the initial procurement for a production-quality ERA in 2003 and has started a process of defining the desired capabilities and requirements for the system.

As part of its preparations for an initial ERA procurement, NARA asked the National Academies' Computer Science and Telecommunications Board (CSTB) to provide independent technical advice on the design of an electronic records archive, including an assessment of how work sponsored by NARA at the San Diego Supercomputer Center (SDSC) helps inform the ERA design and what key issues should be considered in ERA's design and operation.

CSTB's Committee on Digital Archiving and the National Archives and Records Administration has been tasked with preparing two reports. This first of the two reports is intended to provide quick, preliminary feedback to NARA on lessons it should take from the SDSC work and to identify key ERA design issues that should be addressed as the ERA procurement process proceeds in 2003. The committee's second report, anticipated in late 2003, will provide longer-term strategic recommendations to NARA on how to meet its electronic records archiving challenges.

In order to provide feedback as soon as possible, this report has been developed on a very tight time line. In preparing it, the committee received briefings from NARA staff and a number of other experts in archiving and related technologies. It conducted two site visits to supplement information received in the briefings: Members of the committee participated in visits to SDSC in San Diego and to NARA's College Park, Maryland, facility. The committee's second report will provide longer-term strategic recommendations to NARA on how to meet its electronic records archiving challenges. A number of topics in the committee's charter, such as advice on NARA's research program, are deferred to the second report.

Acknowledgment of Reviewers

This report has been reviewed in draft form by individuals chosen for their diverse perspectives and technical expertise, in accordance with procedures approved by the National Research Council's Report Review Committee. The purpose of this independent review is to provide candid and critical comments that will assist the institution in making its published report as sound as possible and to ensure that the report meets institutional standards for objectivity, evidence, and responsiveness to the study charge. The review comments and draft manuscript remain confidential to protect the integrity of the deliberative process. We wish to thank the following individuals for their review of this report:

William Y. Arms, Cornell University,
Eric W. Brown, IBM Research,
Paul Conway, Duke University,
James Gray, Microsoft Bay Area Research Center,
Gary King, Harvard University,
Butler W. Lampson, Microsoft Corporation,
Michael E. Lesk, Internet Archive,
Peter G. Neumann, SRI International,
Jeff Rothenberg, RAND,
William Scherlis, Carnegie Mellon University, and
Jeffrey D. Ullman, Stanford University (emeritus)

Although the reviewers listed above provided many constructive comments and suggestions, they were not asked to endorse the conclusions or recommendations, nor did they see the final draft of the report before its release. The review of this report was overseen by Robert

J. Spinrad, Xerox Corporation (retired). Appointed by the National Research Council, he was responsible for making certain that an independent examination of this report was carried out in accordance with institutional procedures and that all review comments were carefully considered. Responsibility for the final content of this report rests entirely with the authoring committee and the institution.

Contents

SUMMARY AND RECOMMENDATIONS	1
1 INTRODUCTION	13
2 COMMONALITIES BETWEEN REQUIREMENTS FOR THE ERA AND REQUIREMENTS FOR OTHER ACTIVITIES	15
3 SPECIFIC LESSONS TO BE LEARNED FROM THE SDSC DEMONSTRATION PROJECTS	19 |//
Lessons from the SDSC Project That May Be Helpful in Designing the ERA, 20
Aspects of the SDSC Project That Might Not Apply to the NARA System, 22
Areas Where the SDSC Project Experience Should Not Be Used in Designing the NARA System, 23

4 DESIGNING AND ENGINEERING THE ERA 24
An Engineering Approach, 24
Data and Estimates to Support the Definition of Initial Requirements, 25
Pragmatic Engineering Decisions, 26
Supporting Future Archivists and Researchers, 29
Pragmatic Steps to Facilitate Future Access to Records, 30

5 KEY TECHNICAL ISSUES 35
   Data Model, 35
   Storage, 42
   Ingest, 46
   Access, 49
   Security and Access Control, 53
   Integrity of Records, 56

6 STRENGTHENING INFORMATION TECHNOLOGY EXPERTISE 58
   Expertise to Design and Evolve the ERA, 58
   Expertise to Operate the ERA, 60

7 STRATEGY FOR EVOLUTION AND ACQUISITION 62
   Strategy for Evolution, 62
   Iterative (Spiral) Development, 67
   Pilots: Starting Small and Gaining Experience, 68

APPENDIXES

A BACKGROUND ON NARA AND THE ERA PROGRAM 73

B CONCLUSIONS FROM THE GENERAL ACCOUNTING OFFICE REPORT 80
   INFORMATION MANAGEMENT: CHALLENGES IN MANAGING AND PRESERVING ELECTRONIC RECORDS

C BRIEFERS TO THE STUDY COMMITTEE 81

WHAT IS CSTB? 83

Summary and Recommendations

As in other sectors of society, much of the business—and thus record keeping—of the federal government depends on digital information. Documents are created, transmitted, and stored electronically. E-mail has become an important—and often primary—communications technology. And many records exist only in electronic form, stored in databases and other computer systems. Some of these records will, in time, be transferred to the custody of the National Archives and Records Administration (NARA) for long-term preservation.

NARA's current systems for archival preservation of electronic records are limited in capability and ad hoc in nature. Recognizing the growing importance of electronic records to its mission of preserving "essential evidence,"[1] NARA launched the Electronic Records Archives (ERA) initiative. It sponsored work through this program at the San Diego Supercomputer Center (SDSC), which resulted in a series of archival preservation demonstrations. Building on this experience and that of other institutions studying digital preservation, NARA's new ERA Program Office plans to begin initial procurement for a production ERA in 2003. As of this writing, NARA has hired a contractor to assist with the ERA program and has started to define desired capabilities and requirements for the system, including a vision statement and concept of operations for the ERA.

THE IMPORTANCE OF THE ELECTRONIC RECORDS ARCHIVES PROGRAM (CHAPTER 1)

Finding 1. As NARA recognizes, it is critical to start developing new electronic records preservation capabilities quickly in order to continue to fulfill NARA's mandate to preserve federal records.

---

[1] National Archives and Records Administration (NARA). 2000. *Ready Access to Essential Evidence: The Strategic Plan of the United States National Archives and Records Administration 1997-2002* (revised 2002). Government Printing Office, Washington, D.C.

With the rapid increase in federal records in digital form—and with many records born digital or existing only in digital form—it is clear that solutions must be found for preserving these records in order for NARA to continue to fulfill its mandate. NARA has determined and the committee concurs that new capabilities for electronic record archiving are needed for NARA to perform its mission to preserve and provide access to federal records of enduring value.

The overall challenge facing NARA is substantial. The volume and diversity of digital records that will be eligible for transfer from the custody of federal agencies to NARA is projected to be very large. Indeed, it is reasonable to anticipate that in the not-too-distant future, the number of digital records is likely to exceed the number of records originating in paper form. NARA's current systems for electronic records, designed primarily to support preservation of relational databases and similar highly structured records, cannot meet these demands.

The backlog of electronic records presents additional challenges. Under the paper-based model, NARA receives records from a few years to many decades after they were are created. The transfer of electronic records to NARA has for the most part proceeded in similar fashion. Thus when the ERA system becomes operational, NARA will face a large backlog of electronic records that were created over the past few decades, many of which may pose challenging preservation problems owing to their age (media deterioration, loss of documentation and other metadata, and obsolescence of data types). For records yet to be created, there may be ways to avoid the technology obsolescence problem by restructuring records acquisition processes to obtain records closer to the time they are created. (Discussion of this opportunity and related process issues is deferred to the committee's second report.)

If NARA fails to design and implement an electronic records archiving program that is capable of handling the projected volume and diversity of electronic records, important records are likely to be lost for the reasons discussed above. Likewise, significant delays in the ERA program would put records at greater risk of loss. The consequence of either failure to institute a program or a significant delay in doing so would be the possible—indeed even likely—loss of an important part of the nation's history.

Finding 2. ERA systems can and should be built, but it is a challenging, leading-edge engineering undertaking, not a routine procurement.

Although no one has yet designed, built, or managed a production digital archives system on the scale that NARA envisions, the ERA program can be launched in a technically sound way. No off-the-shelf overall solution is available, but there are demonstrated solutions to many of the important system components the ERA will need, making it possible to start building ERA capabilities today. The projected scale and complexity of the ERA program mean that the task of designing, engineering, and evolving the system is a formidable challenge.

Recommendation 1. The ERA should comprise a series of interrelated systems that evolve over time to fulfill NARA's digital preservation needs.

The scope of the ERA in terms of time and function demands that the digital archives be thought of as a set of systems that evolve over time. Digital materials (records and associated metadata) will need to be preserved for a very long time—longer than the lifetime of any physical device or software component that is part of the ERA. This means that hardware and software will have to be replaced or modernized many times without disrupting the archive.

Because requirements for NARA's digital archives will change over time, the ERA systems must be designed to evolve gracefully. For example, new data types (or "file formats"[2]) will emerge and require modifications to parts of the system. Likewise, storage and other implementation technologies will evolve, necessitating the replacement or upgrading of parts of systems without disrupting the operation of the ERA as a whole. The volume of records to be stored will continue to increase, requiring a strategy for graceful scaling of storage and processing. New options for preservation will probably emerge and be incorporated into the ERA. User demands will also change over time, requiring modifications in the ways that records are located and accessed by users.

COMMONALITIES WITH OTHER DIGITAL PRESERVATION ACTIVITIES (CHAPTER 2)

Finding 3. The requirements of NARA's ERA program have much in common with those of other digital preservation systems.

Although NARA's statutory mandate to preserve federal records is unique, many organizations need to preserve digital objects and are taking steps to design and implement systems that address this need. They are developing architectures, techniques, experiments, pilot systems, and expertise relating to digital preservation. NARA has embraced some of these developments, such as the Open Archival Information System (OAIS) reference model for characterizing archival systems in terms of their ingest, storage, and access functions,[3] and is aware of activities in organizations such as the Library of Congress, the National Aeronautics and Space Administration (NASA), and the Online Computer Library Center (OCLC).

The technology to address the ERA largely overlaps the technology required to build other digital repositories. For example, NARA and others require robust long-term storage of bits, accommodation for many different data types, metadata standards and processing techniques, and flexible searching and access provisions. Many systems require a high degree of scalability and the ability to evolve their architecture and implementation. And a number of organizations, government agencies, and businesses also face the challenge of long-term preservation of large volumes of data. As it examines commonalities with others working on digital preservation, NARA should evaluate what is already available as commercial software.

There are a few areas where NARA faces requirements that are more stringent than those typical of other digital repositories. NARA's mandate to guarantee record authenticity is stronger than that of some but not all organizations. NARA must also be ready to preserve materials of very diverse types, even if they were created by obsolete systems or saved on

---

[2]"Data types" is a more general term than "file formats," though the latter may be more familiar.

[3]Consultative Committee for Space Data Systems (CCSDS). 2002. *Reference Model for an Open Archival Information System (OAIS)*, CCSDS 650.0-B-1 (Blue Book). CCSDS Secretariat, National Aeronautics and Space Administration, Washington, D.C. January. Available online at <http://wwwclassic.ccsds.org/documents/pdf/CCSDS-650.0-B-1.pdf>.

obsolete storage media; by contrast, many digital libraries can simplify their challenge by accommodating only a limited set of contemporaneous or common data types. Indeed, the ERA will have to be capable of ingesting the full variety of data types used to create permanent records across the federal government, which will roughly correspond to the full variety of data types in use more broadly. Also, NARA must sometimes redact classified or restricted documents in order to produce versions that can be released to the public. While these and other requirements may be special to NARA's electronic preservation systems, the list of special requirements is modest compared with the list of requirements that the ERA shares with other digital preservation systems.

Recommendation 2. NARA should emphasize the ERA program's commonality with other digital preservation systems and engage with other programs and organizations wherever possible.

NARA would benefit from increased coordination with other federal entities (such as the Library of Congress or NASA), other institutions (such as OCLC, university libraries, archiving projects, and foreign national libraries and archives), and businesses that share common interests in digital preservation. Enhanced coordination should extend at least to increased information sharing as the various institutions move forward with digital repositories. It might extend to such activities as joint work on standards or best practices. However, the committee is not recommending coordinated or joint procurements, which could significantly complicate or delay the ERA program.

It is not enough to be aware of efforts by other institutions; NARA must engage them by becoming an active participant. Engagement means not only that NARA will have better access to the expertise and artifacts that these efforts develop but also that it can influence the research, development, and deployment agendas of these groups when it is appropriate and help build a larger community addressing engineering issues related to digital preservation.

NARA's long-term objective should be to increase the commonalities between its preservation systems and those of other digital repositories such as libraries, because this will (1) make it possible to share software and metadata standards with other institutions, (2) help stimulate the development of commercial off-the-shelf (COTS) components by increasing the size of the market for these components, and (3) help grow the cadre of professionals trained in digital preservation and build ties that would help NARA recruit them to work on the ERA program.

LESSONS LEARNED FROM THE SDSC DEMONSTRATIONS (CHAPTER 3)

Finding 4. Demonstrations conducted at the San Diego Supercomputer Center (SDSC) for NARA have provided a useful opportunity for NARA to explore relevant technologies. However, the work has not informed many significant aspects of the ERA design, has not reduced the engineering risk of the program, and has not enhanced NARA's operational capabilities for running ERA systems.

The SDSC proof-of-concept demonstration projects have provided NARA with the opportunity to interact with the information technology (IT) community and to explore approaches for a production digital archiving system. The SDSC projects have demonstrated options for parts of a production digital archiving system, but NARA should not interpret these projects as solutions to digital archiving issues, as a substitute for gaining experience with operational pilots, or as a source of components of a production system. The areas where the SDSC work falls short of what would be accomplished through operational pilots include the following:

- *Scale.* The quantity of records tested in the SDSC demonstrations is small compared with the quantity of records that NARA anticipates ingesting.
- *Complexity.* The demonstrations addressed only a few relatively simple record types (such as e-mail and Senate legislative records), so the experience is not easily transferable to more complex problems.
- *Attention to trustworthiness issues.* For example, the SDSC work did not address requirements related to redundancy, integrity checks, or access controls.
- *Attention to operational matters.* The SDSC work should be understood as a demonstration of technology rather than as a prototype of an operational system or an operational pilot. The SDSC demonstrations shed little light on the operational issues, such as the work flow associated with ingesting high volumes of varied records, that NARA will need to address in order to run ERA systems. Nor does this exploratory work substitute for having NARA staff work with a system in a production environment; users of SDSC's scientific data management systems, unlike the potential users of the ERA, are generally very savvy about technical matters and can turn to a highly proficient support staff.

Finally, the SDSC work emphasized a particular strategy for digital preservation: migrating records to XML-based formats. Although XML has important applications in archiving, the use of an XML document format does not solve the problem of format obsolescence, and it would be inappropriate to rely on a migration strategy alone for long-term preservation (see Recommendation 4 below). In addition, some aspects of the SDSC demonstrations were research work that attempted to express semantic constraints within records. This is a worthwhile long-term goal that may have some utility as a technique for ingesting or preserving certain types of records. However, this particular demonstration of "lifting knowledge" from a document is not persuasive; the technology is far from ready for inclusion in a production system.

ENGINEERING THE ERA
(CHAPTERS 4 AND 5)

Finding 5. The broad principles and expectations that NARA has established thus far for the ERA are an insufficient basis for proceeding with its design, procurement, and operation.

NARA has thus far expressed the requirements and objectives for the ERA in very high-level terms. Some of these objectives stem directly from its statutory mandate, e.g., "preserve and provide access to any kind of electronic record."[4] It has also embraced the OAIS reference model to describe the high-level structure of the system.

---

[4]The basic goals of NARA and the ERA program, as expressed in NARA documents, are presented in Appendix A of this report.

More preliminary work is required in setting expectations for the system and estimating its size and scope before NARA can start procuring a workable production system. This includes (1) characterizing the electronic records that the ERA should be expected to ingest in the near term and (2) making pragmatic engineering decisions and defining realistic requirements and priorities. Only by jointly considering archival and technical concerns can NARA chart a course to meet its preservation mandate with achievable IT systems.

Recommendation 3. Before proceeding with design and procurement of the ERA, NARA should gather more data about the electronic records that it expects to preserve in the near future.

To formulate some of the quantitative and qualitative requirements of the ERA, NARA needs more information about the population of government records that it will hold and projections about how the records will be used. To guide the engineering of the ERA, and especially of its early versions, NARA should obtain or estimate these data now. None of these attributes will remain unchanged over the life of the system, but it is nonetheless important to develop the system based on these initial requirements.

When data are not available or are impractical to obtain, estimates should be prepared, justified, and made explicit; otherwise, a system design will reflect implicit estimates, which may be dangerously wrong. Importantly, the intent of this recommendation is not that the ERA program should be significantly delayed to conduct detailed surveys; only rough estimates are needed, and order-of-magnitude estimates will suffice in most cases.

Examples of the required data include these:

- *Characterization of the population of digital records that will need to be preserved.* How many government records, using what data types, will require preservation? How many records does NARA expect to receive in each future year? As remarked below, the ERA will need to prioritize handling of records based on archival and technical considerations. Both current data and forward estimates are required in order to make these decisions.
- *Estimates of size and scaling trajectory.* How much data will be stored in the ERA, and how will it grow over time? These estimates, which are needed to inform the technical structure of the system, may follow directly from estimates of the record population but may also be governed by the overall project plan, ingest rates, and other considerations.
- *Mechanisms for delivering records to NARA.* While today's and future records can be delivered to NARA using secure networking techniques, records generated over the past 30 years or less may reside outside network-connected systems on media that are rapidly becoming obsolete. How many records are stored on which media?
- *Estimates of access rates.* Since the ERA does not yet exist, access rates can only be estimated, perhaps based on experience with digital libraries (which might provide a better indication of user interest in online collections than would data on access to NARA's non-electronic records). The system will certainly need to be designed to increase access performance as demand increases, but even an initial system will require some estimate of access rates.
- *Budget estimates.* The quantitative estimates lead to estimates of costs for developing, procuring, and operating the ERA and are critical to making informed design decisions and investment trade-offs. If, for example, it turns out that the originally planned scope of the ERA would be unaffordable, criteria for preservation scheduling may have to be adjusted. Many

design decisions concerning ingest processes and the amount of automation required for them will be driven by the cost of ingesting records of different types. The committee could not find much basis to support estimates for the cost of the ERA, nor could it determine whether current ERA plans are consistent with budgetary constraints.

Recommendation 4. NARA should address key design issues before commencing implementation and apply a pragmatic engineering approach to the ERA's development and evolution.

Although it may be tempting to speak in absolutes (e.g., "every important record will be preserved forever") when designing a system, engineering practice recognizes that there are objectives that are subject to constraints. Engineering the ERA will require specifying the objectives and constraints of such a system.

This report describes and the section below summarizes some of the important design issues that need to be addressed and provides some advice on how to think about them. In some cases, the committee's preliminary analysis led to design suggestions, but this is no substitute for comprehensive analysis by NARA. Key engineering tasks include these:

1. *Prioritize the functions of the ERA and focus initial design on capabilities that permit rapid deployment of operational pilots.* NARA's most basic requirement is to save bits for a hundred years or more. To achieve this requires a combination of careful technical and operational design based on extensive industry experience with robust storage systems of shorter life. Examples of measures to meet this goal are (1) redundant storage of bits at separate physical sites to survive physical destruction, (2) copying bits to new physical storage devices as existing devices age, (3) using storage systems with nonproprietary interfaces to prevent lock-in by any specific vendor, (4) careful system design and operation to guard against human error that might delete vital bits, and (5) diverse system implementations to guard against software errors that could lose data.

One way to gain experience is to build an effective bit storage capability that supports pilot programs to begin preserving records in the short term and that provides a critical foundation for future systems with broader capabilities.

Some basic ingest (i.e., intake of records and associated metadata) and access mechanisms are required in early ERA versions, but other functions that are less important can be deferred for later implementation, as long as the initial architecture, design concept, and implementation strategy are sufficiently flexible and evolvable and sufficient attention has been devoted to overall robustness, survivability, maintainability, and compatibility with critical long-term requirements.

2. *Design for common cases.* Given resource limitations, it is not reasonable to expect a system to preserve and provide equally good support for all records. A relatively small number of data types will likely support the majority of records that federal agencies are creating. It is also advisable that early system builds concentrate on a relatively small number of types. It will be necessary, therefore, to make some choices about what quality of service to provide for different types of record. To decide on the service level accorded each class of record, NARA will need to assess both technical and archival aspects of records. For some lower-priority formats, ERA support should, at least initially, be limited to capturing, storing, and providing access to the original bits and essential metadata.

3. *Take pragmatic steps now to facilitate future access to records.* NARA does not have to anticipate—or invest in—all the higher-level services that future users might want. Indeed, future archivists and researchers will be skilled in computing and thus will be more able to manipulate and interpret digital records. Also, many institutions, including NARA, share an interest in building an infrastructure of tools that support conversion, migration, and emulation; these will be available to NARA and its users.

The ERA should be designed so that certain fundamental information about a record is saved to enable future access. This pragmatic strategy includes the following elements:

- *Be neutral with respect to migration, emulation, or other approaches.* None of today's approaches—such as migration or emulation—for dealing with data type obsolescence have been perfected, nor has one emerged as accepted archival practice. Today, one should rely foremost on saving the original bits—even if one is unable to decode or render those bits when the records are ingested—together with additional information that facilitates their interpretation (preferred derived forms and essential metadata; see below). The viability of whatever strategies are used in the future will depend on the availability of the original bits.
- *Save records in "preferred derived forms" in addition to the original bits.* The derived forms simplify access to records because the formats are chosen pragmatically to be common, well-documented, and expected to last a long time. These derived forms can readily be created for many common record types by making use of existing export functions or conversion software. Derived forms are, however, no substitute for preserving and providing access to the original bits. (A related strategy that may be discussed in the committee's second report is to encourage agencies to create records in preferred formats at the outset.)
- *Do not rely primarily on a strategy of converting records to platform- and vendor-independent archiving formats in an attempt to avoid obsolescence.* This point follows from the previous two elements but is stated explicitly because it runs directly counter to the approach of converting all records to technology-independent formats, which is not likely to be effective. XML formats are often proposed for this role, but they cannot assume the role of the original data type because they cannot be relied on to faithfully encode all of the elements of all data types. By contrast, an XML derived form may be a very useful derived form that serves as an adjunct to saving the original data type.
- *Save essential metadata.* While it is often advisable to save as much metadata as possible, the most important metadata to save are those that cannot be derived from the record itself and thus would otherwise be lost (e.g., contextual metadata).
- *Save essential external references that are implicit or explicit in the record.* Digital files often refer to other digital objects, such as embedded images, tables generated by running some program, and files belonging to other organizations. The possibilities for cross-reference in digital files are far richer than in paper files, and rules will have to be developed to decide which cross-references should be preserved by copy, by reference, or both.
- *Archive as much information as possible about the software and work flow processes used to ingest the original records.* This information may be essential when future users of the archive wish to understand in detail how records have been processed. A desirable goal would be that the ingest process work flow be log-based and otherwise designed to facilitate analysis in case the preserved form of the record is later discovered to have been incorrectly ingested.

4. *Safeguard the bits.* The risks of the various possible causes of data loss—such as malicious acts, natural disasters, software bugs, human error, and hardware failures—should be assessed and used to make informed engineering cost-benefit trade-offs. A combination of appropriate system design and operational policies and procedures will be required. Measures to consider include redundancy (e.g., geographically distributed replicas), media refresh (copying data to new media before old media fail due to age), integrity checks (e.g., to verify the integrity of records received from agencies, to detect errors in data storage systems, and to protect against tampering), access controls (e.g., to control who can write or modify records and to protect classified or otherwise nonpublic records), and auditing. Some records may be deemed more important than others and will justify greater investment than others to ensure that they persist.

5. *Select the appropriate storage media.* The economics, performance, and robustness of all-disk storage systems have recently begun to exceed those of systems that include magnetic tape either as a primary storage medium or as a backup. While not yet common practice, it is likely that robust disk-only storage systems will become an attractive alternative to tape storage early in the life of the ERA. NARA should seriously consider such designs for the first ERA systems; they are much simpler than storage involving both tape and disk. Offline, possibly write-once, storage may continue to play some useful role in storing infrequently accessed records; the cost, complexity, performance, and reliability trade-offs associated with each technology option should be carefully considered. Even if the ERA does not initially eschew tape, it should be designed to make it easy to switch away from tape in the future.

6. *Decide where to invest in access capabilities.* Historically, the primary tool for finding physical (paper) records of interest has been the finding aid; finding aids, along with other surrogate records, are now used by computer systems that help people to find physical records. When the entire contents of digital records are available for computer processing, content-based retrieval techniques like full-text searching (which has proven to be a high-payoff, relatively low-cost method in other contexts) become possible. These will alter access interface designs, ingest, processing, access strategies, cost trade-offs, and even approaches to handling confidential or classified records.

7. *Plan for consistent access to digital and physical records.* Over time, it should become possible to use single, consistent access tools to search all the records in the custody of NARA, be they physical or digital. Indeed, over time, some current physical records may even be transferred to digital form. The ERA design needs to take this into account, and while such cross-collection capabilities would probably not be implemented in early iterations of the ERA, it is essential that the architecture recognize this long-term convergence.

INFORMATION TECHNOLOGY EXPERTISE
(CHAPTER 6)

Finding 6. Greater information technology (IT) expertise is needed if NARA is to successfully design, acquire, and operate ERA systems.

Insufficient technical expertise at NARA is a major obstacle to successful development and acquisition of the ERA. Based on briefings and other interactions with NARA staff, the committee concludes that while there is recognition of the importance of the ERA program, few NARA staff members have experience with or fully understand the complexity of building and managing a program as challenging as the ERA. NARA today does not appear to have sufficient technical depth to assure success in launching the ERA program—that is, to define and manage the overall architecture, develop the appropriate request for proposals, evaluate technical responses, negotiate changes in the architecture with vendors, and manage the implementation of the system.

In addition to needing a quick ramp-up in the IT expertise necessary to oversee the early phases of procurement, NARA faces a longer-term need for a more pervasive culture change— IT skills related to preservation will need to be a core competence throughout the organization, on a par with its other institutional strengths. NARA recognizes the existence of this issue in its appointment of a change manager associated with the ERA program, but the difficulty in achieving this shift cannot be overestimated. It will not be possible to achieve the needed changes quickly; this pervasive change should be addressed in parallel with other facets of ERA development.

Recommendation 5. In order to pursue technical development of the ERA, NARA should first hire a small team of first-rate information technologists with systems design expertise.

The addition of a few employees with properly focused systems design expertise would greatly increase the likelihood that the ERA program will be successful.

Preparing the architectural design of the ERA requires first-class talent having both archival and IT expertise. Whether the architecture is defined by NARA staff (the preferred approach; see Recommendation 7) or contractors, the challenges of hiring qualified IT people are almost identical for these two approaches. If it is to be successful, the contracting approach requires NARA's expertise to equal that of the design contractors in order to determine whether a design will meet NARA's needs.

Contracting for system implementation once an architecture is defined likewise requires at a minimum an in-house contract monitoring staff (e.g., the contracting officer's technical representative) with IT expertise at least as good as that of the contractor's people. This expertise will be essential, in particular if NARA is to successfully pursue an iterative development approach (Recommendation 7).

Recommendation 6. To supplement its in-house expertise, NARA should recruit an advisory group of government, academic, and commercial experts with deep knowledge of digital preservation and IT system design.

A standing ERA advisory committee focused on digital preservation issues would provide an ongoing way to supplement NARA's IT capabilities. By drawing expertise from the range of digital preservation efforts under way in government, industry, and elsewhere, the advisory committee would allow NARA to learn from those efforts and to foster collaboration (e.g., on techniques, standards, or common components) where warranted.

STRATEGY FOR EVOLVING AND ACQUIRING THE ERA
(CHAPTER 7)

Finding 7. Building the ERA as a conventional procurement is unlikely to succeed owing to the difficulty of accurately anticipating all system requirements. Instead, an iterative approach is needed.

Procurement of the ERA is fundamentally different from procurement of a payroll or other commonplace IT system. No one has built an ERA before, and its requirements are not yet completely understood. Also, some of the requirements—such as safeguarding bits with very high confidence—are stringent. As a result, the procurement should emphasize modularity, iteration, and working with vendors to define and evolve the system rather than arms-length specification and delivery of a completed, turnkey system.

The ERA will need to evolve, perhaps rapidly, during its early years as technical and operational requirements are modified by experience. Later in its life, the ERA may evolve more slowly as new needs are identified and as old hardware and software components are replaced or upgraded.

Recommendation 7. The ERA should be designed as a modular system that can be built, maintained, modified, and evolved incrementally, subject to an overall architecture.

A proper modular design allows components to be upgraded without disrupting the operation of the system. An overall structure for the ERA is suggested by the OAIS reference model, but a design for the ERA will need to be much more detailed in order to exploit the benefits of modularity. A modular structure would make it easier to use COTS components for the ERA.

The system's architecture ensures that the pieces fit together, that the system can be incrementally modified, and that it can evolve over time. Interfaces between major parts should be specified using an open approach that allows multiple vendors to supply components over a long lifetime. The architecture is itself subject to evolution over time as requirements are better understood or new requirements emerge. However, devising a good initial architecture is very important as the program's success will be sensitive to the nature of the architectural decisions that are made early on. It is, for example, far harder to evolve the modular structure than to evolve individual modules.

The architecture of the ERA system(s) should be "owned" (specified and evolved over time) by NARA. This would help ensure that NARA understands the implications of alternative proposals, reduces its dependence on vendors and the risk of proprietary lock-in, and understands the limitations and strengths of systems that vendors deliver. Preparing the architectural design of the ERA requires first-class talent having both archival and IT expertise. So too does evolving it over time to meet new requirements.

A far poorer alternative to a NARA-owned architecture is for NARA to contract for one or more architectural designs. In this case, it may be worthwhile to obtain several proposals, because different contractors may have different opportunities or ideas for incorporating COTS elements. This alternative also requires first-class technical talent in order to specify the scope of a design contract, to evaluate resulting designs, and to proceed with acquiring and evolving a system.

Recommendation 8. NARA should begin development of the ERA with a small number of focused pilot production systems designed to gain early experience and to converge ultimately into a smaller number of more comprehensive systems.

NARA should concurrently develop and deploy small, focused systems that rapidly build operational experience. All of these systems should be built within a common architectural framework (Recommendation 7), so that they may eventually coalesce into a smaller number of more comprehensive systems as experience and confidence grow. It is especially important that the data model—the data types and related metadata—conform to the architecture so that the digital data obtained by ingesting records into one of the early systems will carry forward into future evolutions.

The initial systems should be selected and scoped for rapid deployment—this is the key to gaining early experience to inform the requirements of later systems. The following are some examples of limited-scope systems that might be considered for early pilots:

- *U.S. State Department diplomatic cables.* NARA is preparing to acquire a collection of diplomatic cables, which are simple structured text files, in digital form. Ingest might include automatic extraction of metadata from the cables; access might include full-text search or other methods appropriate to the collection. For quickest deployment, NARA might consider making these records available using software already developed for operating a digital library.
- *Records at the National Personnel Records Center.* There is interest in preserving large but homogeneous collections of official military records scanned in TIFF image format when they are transferred to NARA's National Personnel Records Center. Confidentiality considerations and the imperative to provide ready access to veterans or next-of-kin would require careful attention to access controls.
- *E-mail from the Clinton administration held by the Clinton Presidential Center.* Metadata could be extracted from the e-mail headers, full-text search could be provided, and so on. The presence of attachments would permit gaining experience with preserving and providing access to a broad range of relatively contemporary data types.

These three examples illustrate collections that could be organized and made available quickly. Although these collections might lack the scale of the eventual ERA, early deployment of systems to preserve and access them would yield important operational experience for NARA and avoid costly mistakes in later, more complex systems.

Experience with early systems can be expected to lead to changes to the ERA architecture and to the substantial refinement of requirements for subsequent, more comprehensive systems. Managing the initial architecture, the first system deployments, the learning from early operations, and the revisions to architecture and specifications, and evolving the ERA will be the task of NARA's augmented IT staff.

1

Introduction

With the rapid increase in federal records originating in digital form (including word processing documents, e-mail messages, images, and database records), it is very clear that solutions must be found for preserving these records in order for NARA to fulfill its mandate. In fact, as NARA itself recognizes, its strategic future depends on the development of a suitable archive for electronic records. In the not-too-distant future, the total number of born-digital records—and the number of those that are permanently valuable—may well exceed the number that originate in paper form. The flow of digital records into NARA will be enormous. Compounding the challenge, the backlog of existing digital records when NARA systems for archiving them become operational will be large.

NARA launched the Electronic Records Archives (ERA) initiative in the late 1990s, envisioning that it would "authentically preserve and provide access to any kind of electronic record."[1] NARA's new ERA Program Office plans to commence the initial procurement for the ERA in 2003. As of this writing, NARA has hired a contractor to assist with the ERA program and has started a process of defining desired capabilities and requirements for the system, including the development of a vision statement and concept of operations for the ERA. Further background on NARA and the ERA program can be found in Appendixes A and B.

ERA's broad objectives for archiving digital records build on NARA's extensive experience in archiving paper records. But digital records present new problems—and opportunities—with very little operational experience for guidance. In some ways, digital records improve on paper—they can, for example, be easily searched and delivered electronically and it is cheap to keep more than one copy in case one is destroyed. But digital records are

---

[1] Electronic Records Program Office, National Archives and Records Administration (NARA ERA PMO). 2002. *Electronic Records Archives Vision Statement.* NARA ERA PMO, Washington, D.C. April 18.

vulnerable to new forms of loss, such as tampering, storage failures, obsolescence of data types, and failure to archive all the data required to reconstitute a record. Finally, researchers—especially in the future—will use electronic records quite differently from paper records. The design and operation of the ERA must anticipate the differences between paper and electronic records but also be prepared to change as the requirements of an electronic records archive become clearer.

NARA's current systems for electronic records archiving are limited in capability and ad hoc in nature. NARA does have some useful foundations to build on. The Open Archival Information System (OAIS) reference model[2] offers a good conceptual design, including a very-high-level modularity. But design and implementation must go well beyond the generalities of an OAIS model. NARA has also gained some experience in the application of digital archiving tools through its work with the San Diego Supercomputer Center (SDSC). NARA-sponsored work at SDSC resulted in the development of a system and set of tools that were used to conduct a series of archiving demonstrations.[3] Some useful lessons can be drawn from this work (see Chapter 3). The primary design challenges facing NARA relate not to the development of fundamental technologies but to addressing a number of engineering issues surrounding the building of these systems (Chapters 4 and 5) and an evolvable system architecture and strategy for managing the ongoing evolution of the ERA (Chapter 7). Other challenges relate to the IT expertise required for the ERA's design and operation and cultural changes associated with the growing importance of digital records in both NARA and federal agencies (see Chapter 6).

The committee strongly endorses the concept of an ERA. Such a system can and should be designed and implemented. Building such a system is critical to NARA's mission, and NARA should move forward as quickly as possible to start developing these capabilities. But, as the committee shows in the chapters that follow, many areas will need attention if the program is to be successful.

---

[2]Consultative Committee for Space Data Systems (CCSDS). 2002. *Reference Model for an Open Archival Information System (OAIS)*. CCSDS 650.0-B-1 (Blue Book). CCSDS Secretariat, National Aeronautics and Space Administration, Washington, D.C. January. Available online at <http://wwwclassic.ccsds.org/documents/pdf/CCSDS-650.0-B-1.pdf>.

[3]A detailed description of this work is provided in Reagan Moore, 2001, *Final Report for the Research Project on Application of Distributed Object Computation Testbed Technologies to Archival Preservation and Access Requirements*, San Diego Supercomputer Center (SDSC) Technical Report TR-2001-8, SDSC, San Diego, Calif., available online at <http://www.sdsc.edu/TR/TR-2001-08.doc.pdf>. A number of additional technical reports on this work are available at the project Web site <http://www.sdsc.edu/NARA/Publications.html>. Briefer descriptions can be found in Reagan Moore et al., 2000, "Collection-Based Persistent Digital Archives - Part 1," *D-Lib Magazine* 6(2), March, available online at <http://www.dlib.org/dlib/march00/moore/03moore-pt1.html> and Reagan Moore et al., 2000, "Collection-Based Persistent Digital Archives - Part 2," *D-Lib Magazine* 6(4), April, available online at <http://www.dlib.org/dlib/april00/moore/04moore-pt2.html>.

2

Commonalities Between Requirements for the ERA and Requirements for Other Activities

The committee heard repeatedly in briefings by NARA staff that NARA's requirements are unique. This perspective is found in numerous articles, position statements, and requirements documents related to the ERA program.[1] It is based on the idea that special requirements apply to archival institutions, that NARA plays a unique role in the federal government, and that the scale and diversity of the government's programs exceed those of any other entity. NARA does have unique statutory responsibilities for the management of federal government records and the identification and preservation of records of long-term value. However, its situation is in many respects not all that different from that of many other organizations that also have mandates to preserve digital information.

It would be a mistake to start with the position that (1) NARA's requirements are unique and (2) preserving records is fundamentally different from preserving other types of information. Such an assumption would limit NARA's potential to benefit from common solutions to archiving challenges found throughout the federal government and other organizations with long-term preservation needs. State and local governments face many of the same problems, as does the private sector. Moving away from the position that NARA's requirements are unique would also open up many possibilities for closer collaboration between NARA and other organizations with similar archiving challenges. The benefits of common solutions and collaboration would include these:

- *Freeing up development resources to tackle more exceptional problems.* To the extent that NARA can make use of common (including off-the-shelf) options for such components as

---

[1]See, e.g., Kenneth Thibodeau, 2001, "Building the Archives of the Future," *D-Lib Magazine*, 7(2), February. Available online at <http://www.dlib.org/dlib/february01/thibodeau/02thibodeau.html>; and NARA, 2002, *Electronic Records Archives Feature List*, ERA Program Office, NARA, October 31.

storage and data management, resources will be available to solve more specialized problems such as ingest of and access to unusual record formats.

- *Reducing development costs.* To the extent that commonalities are identified, NARA's development costs can be reduced by increasing the potential size of the market for archiving system components. Development costs would also be reduced by collaborative work on common tools (e.g., format conversion, automatic ingest, and metadata extraction and mark-up), standards (e.g., metadata standards and key interfaces to modules), and other technologies for preservation.
- *Easing ingest.* To the extent that NARA can build a repository on common standards, it will make it easier for federal agencies to deposit digital materials in a NARA repository or for NARA to harvest records worthy of preservation.
- *Facilitating interoperability.* Adoption of common standards by NARA and other institutions will facilitate the development of federated collections by third parties and enable users to employ common tools across multiple digital repositories.
- *Transferring benefits from NARA's experience and investments to a larger community and vice versa.* NARA's participation in developing and disseminating information about the OAIS model and its work with the group developing the Metadata Encoding and Transmission Standard (METS) are good examples.
- *Sharing technical expertise and knowledge.* Both formal and informal mechanisms can be used to tap outside knowledge of and experience with digital archiving. As discussed in Chapter 6, IT expertise is critical to the success of the ERA program.
- *Identifying and recruiting new IT talent.* More collaboration will increase the opportunities to identify new IT talent to design and implement the ERA program. For example, a number of graduate students are being trained in digital libraries.

Recent research and development activities in digital preservation have emphasized defining archiving problems in as generic a way as possible and seeking solutions that are common to the many types of organizations with long-term preservation needs.[2] The collection-based persistent archive model developed at SDSC (with support from NARA), for example, seeks solutions to digital preservation by integrating archival storage technology from supercomputer centers, data grid technology from the scientific community, information models from digital libraries, and preservation models from the archival community. The SDSC persistent archive prototype (discussed in Chapter 3) aims to support long-term preservation of collections from scientific data repositories, large digital libraries, and archives with the same architecture. NARA also contributed to the development and dissemination efforts of

---

[2]See, for example, Commission on Preservation and Access and Research Library Group (RLG), 1996, *Preserving Digital Information: Final Report and Recommendations*, RLG, Mountain View, Calif., May, available online at <http://www.rlg.org/ArchTF/>; CEDARS Metadata Standards, available online at <http://www.leeds.ac.uk/cedars/index.html>; RLG-OCLC Working Group on Digital Preservation Metadata, 2002, *Trusted Digital Repositories: Attributes and Responsibilities* (an RLG-OCLC report), RLG, Mountain View, Calif., May, available online at <http://www.rlg.org/longterm/repositories.pdf>; and various documents from the Digital Preservation Coalition, available online at <http://www.dpconline.org/>.

the Consultative Committee on Space Data Systems, which developed the OAIS reference model, which is now an international standard.[3] The OAIS reference model provides common terminology and a high-level framework for an archive.[4]

Many other groups, including these, are working on long-term digital preservation issues:

- *Library of Congress (LoC)*. Through the National Digital Information Infrastructure and Preservation Program, LoC is developing a repository for LoC's own digital collections (both born-digital and turned-digital); developing standards and mechanisms for the exchange of preserved digital objects; and working toward mechanisms for interoperability among digital repositories. Like NARA, LoC is seeking more efficient methods for acquiring digital collections in many different formats, working to identify metadata standards for access and intellectual property rights management, and seeking technology for a repository system.
- *National archives and libraries in other countries*. The Netherlands' Koninklijke Bibliotheek (KB) has built on the work of a European collaborative project, Nedlib, to build a system to store KB's collection of born-digital documents.[5] IBM is implementing the system drawing on a number of off-the-shelf products.
- *Digital library researchers*. This research community addresses issues such as storage and data management of large amounts of information in diverse formats and media (e.g., text, images, video, music, recorded speech); search within a single archive using controlled-vocabulary and/or content-based indexing; federated search across collections, including collections operated by different organizations; metadata conversion; format conversion; resource (archive) selection; and interoperability among archives.
- *Digital library operators*. Much practical experience has been gained by the operators of such digital libraries as the California Digital Library, JSTOR, the National Library of Medicine, and the Library of Congress.
- *Federal agencies*. Some federal agencies, including the National Aeronautics and Space Administration, the National Institutes of Health (especially the National Library of Medicine), the Department of Defense, and the intelligence agencies already manage large digital repositories.
- *State and local governments*. State and local governments also maintain archives and thus face long-term preservation challenges quite similar to those of NARA.
- *Private sector*. Online text retrieval services such as Lexis-Nexis and WestLaw maintain very large digital libraries. A number of industry sectors, such as pharmaceuticals, public utilities, aviation, and those using hazardous materials, must retain very large collections of records for the long term to fulfill regulatory requirements.

---

[3]Consultative Committee for Space Data Systems (CCSDS). 2002. *Reference Model for an Open Archival Information System (OAIS)*. CCSDS 650.0-B-1 (Blue Book). CCSDS Secretariat, National Aeronautics and Space Administration, Washington, D.C. January. Available online at <http://wwwclassic.ccsds.org/documents/pdf/CCSDS-650.0-B-1.pdf>.

[4]The model does not provide the specifications for a particular architecture or an implementation framework; it does define core functions as ingest, archival storage, data management, access, administration, and preservation planning.

[5]See <http://www.kb.nl/dnep-project>.

In summary, NARA's requirements for many aspects of the ERA—such as archival storage, data management, preservation, administration, and preservation planning—are surprisingly similar to the requirements of any other organization preserving digital data for the long term. NARA has much to gain by starting from the premise of common requirements in these areas first and then clearly specifying where its requirements are different or unique.

3

Specific Lessons to Be Learned from the SDSC Demonstration Projects

Starting in 1998, NARA cosponsored work at the San Diego Supercomputer Center (SDSC) to explore the long-term preservation of electronic records. Recently, NARA and the National Science Foundation (NSF) have been supporting work to extend and refine an architecture developed at SDSC and now referred to as "persistent archives."

SDSC is part of the National Partnership for Advanced Computational Infrastructure (NPACI), a collaboration among 46 U.S. member institutions and foreign affiliates. The principal thrust of this collaboration is to develop the computational infrastructure required to support large-scale scientific computation. The partnership has developed techniques to link together large computers into a global grid, and a corresponding data grid for storing numerous large data sets used in scientific computation.

SDSC has considerable experience building and operating large data storage systems. The current data archive has a capacity of about 400 TB, in which tape robots move data between tape cartridges of roughly 20 GB capacity and a 1.6-TB disk cache. A high-speed network gateway delivers up to 90 MB/sec transfer rates to computational nodes via networks of various kinds. This system is designed principally for high capacity and the very-high-speed access required by supercomputers.

SDSC has also developed data management techniques that allow uniform access to files from different kinds of computer systems. Principal among these is the Storage Request Broker (SRB), which mediates between clients and storage of various kinds (file systems, databases, and the tape archive). Files are accessed by a logical name; the SRB middleware determines where files are stored and how to access them. Also kept is a metadata catalog, which principally records file metadata (such as the location of a file), but may also contain application- or domain-specific metadata. Several SRBs may work in concert to form a federated data management system, in which clients access the combined collections of the federation. These facilities have the important property that they hide computer- and vendor-dependent details, so that storage equipment can be upgraded without changing client software.

They are routinely used by scientific computing applications: Organizing and saving scientific datasets for a long time is an important requirement for NPACI users.

For its NARA work, SDSC has built a number of demonstrations that use this data-storage infrastructure.[1] The archival processing conforms to the OAIS model, with its principal ingest, storage, and access components. The demonstrations have treated a few record collections, building ingest and access functions suitable for each. A few examples follow:

- Approximately a million electronic mail messages were ingested. Header fields, such as sender, recipient, date, and subject, were extracted to form metadata for each message. Messages were transformed into an XML representation to explicitly tag the metadata elements. A relational database of metadata allowed easy retrieval of messages based on metadata properties—e.g., all messages from a given sender on a given day. This experiment did not attempt to deal with e-mail attachments and their wide-ranging data types.
- Files describing the Senate Legislative Activities for the 106th Congress, expressed as 99 Rich Text Format (RTF) files, were ingested. These files were created from an IT system (the Thomas system) that keeps track of bills, amendments, and resolutions for each senator. The SDSC project attempted to "lift knowledge" from the text representation to obtain something akin to the original database, by first converting from RTF to an XML format, then (in effect) parsing text to extract names of senators, committees, bills, etc. This work showed inconsistencies in the original database (especially the omission of one senator from the collection). The result was expressed as a (new) database using XML syntax.
- An electronic database already held in NARA archives describing air missions over Vietnam was transformed into an XML format for preservation. One problem that required attention was normalizing several coordinate systems, including a military grid scheme no longer in use. In the process of building presentation tools, SDSC discovered inconsistencies in the geographic (and geometric) data in the database. Expressing the map data in XML permitted building quite simple presentation viewers using commercial tools.

All of these demonstrations stressed the use of XML as a preservation format because of its independence from vendor- or computer-system specifics, in some cases taking advantage of freeware or commercial packages for processing XML.

In the remainder of this chapter, the committee assesses the usefulness of certain strategies and features of the SDSC work and classifies them as (1) lessons that might influence the construction of the NARA system, (2) aspects that may not apply, and (3) choices that NARA should not consider. These specific lessons complement the engineering issues discussed in the succeeding chapters.

LESSONS FROM THE SDSC PROJECT THAT MAY BE HELPFUL IN DESIGNING THE ERA

1. *The SDSC work increases confidence that it is possible to build an electronic archive system and that some of the assumptions behind the project are sound.* The SDSC project demonstrated both

---

[1]Reagan Moore. 2002. "The San Diego Project: Persistent Objects," *Proceedings of the Workshop on XML as a Preservation Language*, Urbino, Italy, October. Available online at <http://www.sdsc.edu/NARA/Publications.htm>.

archival and technical processes for embedding a few of NARA's electronic collections within a prototype electronic archive. In particular, the demonstrations showed the following:

- The OAIS model provides a useful overall system structure, although it does little to help specify an implementation. The basic OAIS structure—ingest, storage, and access—was successfully mirrored in the overall modular design of the SDSC demonstrations.
- XML is a useful way to represent metadata.
- A significant degree of independence from particular vendors and systems can be achieved.

The SDSC demonstrations also show how modern networking technologies can be used to interconnect heterogeneous machines and to add equipment as needed to increase capacity. Networking technologies also allow parts of the system to be physically separated. The XAPT ingest workbench demonstrated by SDSC can be operated anywhere—for example, run on workstations in the agency that originates the records even though other parts of the work flow, and the archival storage, are located elsewhere.

2. *Metadata sets will be constantly changing.* The writings of the electronic archive community make it clear that a universal metadata set is extremely unlikely. The SDSC projects exploited the ability to tailor metadata sets for each collection. The scientific data sets that SDSC archives make even more extensive and critical use of metadata (e.g., recording important physical parameters of instruments used to make measurements that are recorded in the file) than is likely in an archive of electronic government records.

3. *Indexing metadata offers a simple and effective way to search for archived records.* The SDSC system entered pertinent metadata into a relational database, which could be searched to locate records. This approach leverages the power of relational database systems, including interactive query software, and is easy to understand and use. Metadata searches are not as powerful as full-text searches, but the SDSC work demonstrated their value.

4. *Placing a "federation layer" between the archival system and its file storage is a very useful technique, and the SDSC implementation of such a layer (the SRB) is quite extensive.* The SRB is a piece of middleware that enables distributed clients to access storage resources in a heterogeneous environment. Among the benefits of the SRB approach, the following are particularly noteworthy:

- The SRB approach provides uniform access to and manipulation of files stored in file systems, databases, and archival storage.
- It allows new implementations of file systems (or storage types) to be added to the system as it evolves. This allows storage capacity to increase; it also allows new hardware to be introduced. However, the SRB does not provide automatic refreshing—copying of data from old storage equipment to new—which would be a desirable capability in a production system.
- Similarly, it allows unused file systems to be removed.
- It supports location-independent access to files by keeping a mapping between the permanent file identifier and the physical location of the file.

- It allows working files to be accessible in exactly the same fashion that archived files are. This means that a collection can be tested before it is committed to the archive ("tested" may mean that audits are performed to ensure integrity or to verify that the access software works correctly). In other words, the same auditing and access software can access collections as works in progress as well as archived collections.
- Very-high-speed data transfer rates can be provided if necessary.

5. *The project demonstrated several successful uses of significant COTS products.* COTS file system implementations (hardware and software) are easily incorporated using SRB mediation. Commercial relational database software maintains a metadata index and processes ad hoc queries used to find records in the archive.

ASPECTS OF THE SDSC PROJECT THAT MIGHT NOT APPLY TO THE NARA SYSTEM

1. *The SDSC file system's exclusive use, at least for long-term archival, of off-line tape storage.* Tape is clearly not the only way to build a robust, long-term file system, and a trend toward increased use of online disk storage is evident. Tape storage propagates significant complexity to the rest of the system, especially the requirement that efficient use of tape requires files to be quite large—a minimum of several gigabytes. The trade-offs between tapes and other media depend significantly on how often and in what patterns the data are accessed. Since the SDSC demonstrations made no attempt to mimic the scale of an operating ERA, they offer no evidence that tape archival storage will have adequate performance.

2. *The conversion of each record to a single XML representation as a way to achieve persistence— i.e., to avoid obsolescence of data types.* SDSC's approach to persistence of data types relies on the conversion of records into an XML representation as part of the ingest process. This method has a number of problems. For example, there is no mention of how a stylesheet specification might be archived and remain executable in the future. Style sheets refer to an underlying rendering model that may change with time; moreover, the existing standards for style sheets do not cover all possible rendering and presentation techniques. An example helps make this more concrete: One can instruct Microsoft Word to produce HTML or XML, but the output will contain many Word-specific tags. If these tags are not understood, one has access to the text but may lose access to a lot of information about layout, change tracking, and many other things.

Also, the SDSC project demonstrated the XML approach only for simple record formats, such as electronic mail messages, and tackled neither complex—but increasingly common— commercial record types, such as presentations with animation, nor the issues associated with preserving records that contain scripts or executable elements.

3. *Validation of approaches through use in a production environment or for an extended period of time.* Because the SDSC demonstrations were limited in scope and duration, they do not provide the same sort of operational experience that would be gained from operating early iterations of an ERA. For example, no provision was made for automated media refresh (automatically copying bits from an aging storage medium to a newer one). Nor did the

demonstrations address the problems of work flow and scale associated with ingest—for example, How will NARA be able to ingest electronic records fast enough to meet its needs?

The SDSC demonstrations also shed little light on the operational capabilities NARA will need to run ERA systems. ERA users are less likely to have such skills or recourse to the same sort of IT support. Each demonstration was carried out by highly skilled programmers capable of diagnosing problems in the input documents, the ingest processing, and the data finally added to the archive. There was no attempt to build a system for ingest that could be operated on a routine basis by less skilled people. (Users of SDSC's scientific data management systems are generally highly technically savvy and they can turn to a highly proficient support staff.) More generally, such exploratory work is no substitute for having NARA staff work with a system in a production environment.

AREAS WHERE THE SDSC PROJECT EXPERIENCE SHOULD NOT BE USED IN DESIGNING THE NARA SYSTEM

1. *The archival file system used, HPSS, should not be used as a model for NARA because it lacks important properties.* HPSS is designed for manipulating large data sets on large computers (i.e., scientific data on supercomputers), which have a set of requirements different from those of an electronic archive. For example, HPSS does not provide facilities for replication (redundant copies must be created explicitly), for automatically refreshing the storage media (media refresh has been done under HPSS, but it requires explicit management by staff), or for geographic redundancy.

2. *The SDSC project covered a very small number of file formats and cannot therefore serve as a model for preserving records across the federal government, where a large number of formats will be encountered.* The project, for example, did not consider the following:

- How to prioritize how much support to provide to which formats (quality of service),
- How to determine what subset of formats may cover many of the commonly found record types, and
- How to deal with formats for which there are no existing tools to extract the information from which an XML structure can be built.

3. *The efforts to build a knowledge layer are not ready for deployment.* Trying to express semantic constraints within records is a worthwhile long-term goal, but the demonstrations of how to "lift knowledge" from a document (such as the Senate legislative activity example discussed above) is not persuasive. These techniques are insufficiently developed to be planned for the NARA system.

4

Designing and Engineering the ERA

AN ENGINEERING APPROACH

The ERA program is a complex undertaking. Its archiving goals for the ERA program are ambitious, in keeping with NARA's tradition of careful stewardship of the records it preserves. To meet these goals the ERA will have to be engineered properly. Key elements of an engineering approach include expressing program objectives and constraints, measuring or estimating key parameters, defining realistic requirements, and making pragmatic engineering design decisions. This chapter discusses these issues in the context of the ERA program. The two chapters that follow address design issues related to key system properties, including scalability, reliability, trustworthiness, and longevity.

Attention to engineering principles is especially important because the work done by NARA to date, as evidenced in the documents and briefings provided to the committee, displays insufficient engineering perspective. Efforts to date have focused on articulating high-level preservation requirements, an essential early step for developing the system's archival requirements. However, in order to develop a procurement plan through which successive iterations of working systems can be built, delivered, and made operational in a reasonable amount of time, NARA will have to address the specific engineering considerations and cost trade-offs that this section discusses.

Engineering practice depends strongly on experience with prior designs. In this case, there is no body of prior designs from which to draw direct lessons—no large-scale, long-lived, wide-scope electronic archives exist today. Instead, one must seek experience in the engineering portions of other systems that have properties required of the ERA and gain experience by building capabilities incrementally. For example, copious experience is available for important elements of the ERA system, e.g., a scalable, robust file system. Other qualities, such as very-long-term preservation, can be shaped by experience in the industry, even if there is scant experience with systems designed explicitly to preserve for the very long term. Finally,

DATA AND ESTIMATES TO SUPPORT THE DEFINITION OF INITIAL REQUIREMENTS

Engineering for the ERA program requires a solid understanding of requirements, including the data types[1] to be accommodated, the quantity of records to be stored, the kinds of access to be provided, and the performance expected. Although these requirements can be expected to evolve at every stage of a system's life as a result of changes in the characteristics of electronic records, the system will successfully meet its expectations only if its engineering is in step with its requirements. So it is essential, even for the very first system, to state these requirements carefully and explicitly.

A key to understanding the initial requirements is information about the population of government records that it will hold and projections about how those records will be used. Importantly, great precision is not needed. Indeed, in some cases, data may be unavailable or impractical to obtain. It is not necessary to significantly delay the ERA program in order to conduct in-depth surveys. Rough, even order-of-magnitude estimates, if well justified, will suffice in most cases.

It is important that estimates supporting initial requirements be made explicit; otherwise, a system design might reflect implicit estimates that are dangerously wrong. The assumptions and reasoning behind the estimates should be made explicit. This will allow the estimates and consequent decisions to be modified whenever the assumptions and estimates change.

In order for the first iterations of the ERA to be designed, questions such as the following need to be answered:

- *What are the data types that it must support, and what is their frequency of occurrence?* In what forms do records currently exist—e.g., which data types, on what storage media, and with what kinds of supporting documentation or online metadata? If there is an inventory of digital records "waiting in the wings" to be archived, what are the properties of these collections? The system design must also anticipate and accommodate new data types and changes in their distribution over time.
- *How much data must be accommodated at the outset?* A great many design decisions (such as the archive media, the implementation technology, and the techniques used to provide reliability) will require estimates of the scale of the archive. The committee heard estimates of

---

[1] Throughout this report, "data type" is used to identify the data-encoding rules whereby various kinds of records (documents, electronic mail messages, pictures, database entries, etc.) are expressed as a collection of bits. Thus an image might be represented by bits whose data type is TIFF or GIF or JPEG or any of a number of other such specifications. "File format" is often used interchangeably with "data type," but "data type" is used throughout this report because the literal interpretation of "file format" is files of bits, which would be too restricted. For example, when an image is embedded in an e-mail message that is itself embedded in a "folder" of many messages saved in a file, the bits representing the image cannot properly be called a "file."

1 PB, but this figure needs to be verified and justified. What is the expected rate at which the archive will need to scale? Is the initial flow into the archive likely to be a small number of very large files or a very large number of small files or some combination of these?

- *How will the records be delivered to NARA?* While today's and future records can be delivered to NARA using secure networking techniques, records generated over the past 30 years or less may reside on media that are rapidly becoming obsolete. How many records are stored on which media? Early versions of the ERA may have a disproportionately greater burden to deal with old media. Alternatively, NARA might decide to contract for media conversion services to copy the data to modern media. In any case, an inventory of media types and quantities is required.
- *What rates of access to the archive will be required?* Access rate might be measured by counting retrieved documents per day, retrieved gigabytes per day, searches per day, or all three. How will NARA provide for searching, retrieval, and access in the digital archive? Will users be able to search and retrieve files and items online? Will NARA be able to support search across and within individual record groups and series? Will there be provisions for full-text search? Will such services be provided by NARA or third parties? Estimating access requirements in advance will seem very difficult, and it will surely change as the archive grows, but an initial estimate is essential to produce the first system implementation.
- *What financial resources are available, and how much will it cost to acquire and operate the system?* No engineering project can be undertaken without some expectation of its costs. Back-of-the-envelope calculations can be done to estimate how much computer and storage equipment will be required, the cost of personnel to ingest records and operate the system, and the cost of building the system software. Of particular concern is the cost of manual processes required to ingest records, especially manually recording metadata for records. Because it is not a routine procurement, it is difficult today to project the eventual costs of building and operating a full-scale system, but it is nonetheless important to estimate costs of the early iterations. Experience with each iteration should be used to help inform cost estimates for future versions.
- *Technology lifespan.* At what rate are components such as storage devices expected to be replaced? What is the unit of replacement?

The committee has seen scant evidence that questions of this sort have been posed carefully or answered with enough rigor thus far to set the stage for procuring ERA systems.

PRAGMATIC ENGINEERING DECISIONS

While it can be tempting to deal in absolutes when designing a system ("every important record will be preserved forever"), engineering practice recognizes that a system is designed to meet objectives subject to constraints. A bridge has a limited load capability, traffic capacity, lifetime, and budget. Engineering for the ERA will similarly require expressing its objectives and constraints. This will require some "engineering" considerations not often found in writing about archival processes:

1. *Design for common cases.* Although the archive has an obligation to save every record scheduled for preservation, a different quality of service can be applied to different records. Service-level differentiation is a practical necessity. It is not feasible to delay system develop-

ment until a solution is developed for every conceivable record type (and no universal solution is on the horizon that would apply across record types and thus significantly reduce the incremental cost of handling new record types). The alternative, a strategy whereby agencies would be required to submit documents in specific data types, would put a burden on the agencies that could mean that some records of historical value would not be preserved. If NARA were to insist on a uniform level of service for all record formats, then the level of service in the ERA probably would reduce to the lowest common denominator.

The strategy "accept everything; provide different quality of access" ensures that all records are captured and leaves NARA the opportunity to provide enhanced access in the future as technology improves. There is a trade-off here: Access may, in fact, become more difficult over time as data types become obsolete, but one does not want to wait until more robust access functionality is available before taking steps to capture and preserve records. For example, more compute power, better conversion tools or emulators, or other technological advances might make accessing some records feasible in the future even though it is not feasible today. The quality-of-service approach leaves that option available without jeopardizing the construction or utility of a first system.

Service-level differentiation means that NARA may accept and preserve records in any data type, but certain access services will simply not be available for certain data types. Some records will be accessed more than others; some by the public, some only by scholarly researchers. It may not be cost-effective for NARA to provide online access facilities for obscure data types, but users should be able to retrieve the original bits and use their own resources to manipulate them.

For example, it is perfectly reasonable that NARA might be able to easily provide full-text search capabilities for some types of record but not for others.[2] Another example: NARA might fairly easily provide services for viewing, manipulating, and copying a set of maps stored in common bitmapped image formats, while it might not offer such capabilities for maps embedded in a proprietary geographical information system. Once the notion of service level differentiation is accepted, it can become a powerful approach for simplifying system design.

One way to establish priorities is frequency of occurrence: Although the total universe of possible record data types is very large, a large fraction of NARA's preservation needs can be met by devoting significant effort to the most commonly used data types. Assessments by archivists of significance or likelihood of access might be other ways to prioritize record types.

NARA should therefore focus on commonly used data types and acknowledge that by explicit design, documents in commonly used data types will be preserved with a higher quality of access service.[3] As a result, an early step in the design process should be a survey

---

[2]One example where full-text would be harder to support is records available only in bitmapped image format. However, applying optical character recognition can often recover searchable text from scanned documents. And a variety of research is under way to search collections of pictures for certain features, e.g., images of people. As part of its service-level definitions, NARA will decide whether to offer such services. As the ERA evolves, more such services are likely to be offered.

[3]NARA's recent development of guidance for transfer of records in three common formats—PDF, TIFF, and e-mail with attachments—is a good example of identifying and placing priority on common data types. See National Archives and Records Administration (NARA), 2002, Transfer of Permanent E-records to NARA, NARA, College Park, Md. Available online at <http://www.archives.gov/records_management/initiatives/transfer_to_nara.html>.

or well-justified estimate (based, perhaps, on sampling) of the data types used in digital records found throughout the federal government as well as records already in NARA custody. From the survey, data types can be prioritized based on frequency of occurrence and other criteria.

2. *Prioritize the functions of the ERA and focus initial design on capabilities that permit rapid deployment of operational pilots.* Which capabilities must the ERA have from the outset? Which can be added later?

A key requirement is to save bits for a hundred years or more. To achieve this requires a combination of careful technical and operational design based on extensive industry experience with robust storage systems of shorter life (see Chapter 5). An effective bit storage capability is required for any pilot program and provides a critical foundation for future systems with broader capabilities.

In addition to storage, certain ingest and access mechanisms are required in early ERA versions. However, as discussed above, it may be acceptable for collections to be correctly ingested but for access to them to be primitive at first, improving only later as new access functions are added to the system. Other functions that are less important can be deferred for later implementation, as long as the initial architecture, design concept, and implementation strategy are sufficiently flexible and evolvable and have devoted sufficient attention to overall robustness, survivability, maintainability, and compatibility with critical long-term requirements. Later iterations of the ERA might include additional migration, emulation, or other preservation functionality as these technologies become more mature.

It may also be prudent to set priorities that determine the order in which records are added to the growing archive. These priorities might be similar to those used to establish quality of service, e.g., common record types are ingested first. Record types that are used infrequently or difficult to process may be deferred.

This prioritization of functions can be helpful in other contexts. Suppose that at some later point in time, funding for the ERA were to be curtailed (e.g., due to extreme budget pressures). Which functions would it need to continue to operate, and which could be reduced?

3. *Support a division of labor.* Must NARA build the entire ERA or might other government organizations, commercial firms, and individual researchers fulfill parts of the ERA's mission? The committee recommends that NARA define its *essential* mission quite narrowly, with an emphasis on saving digital records in their original form together with appropriate metadata and providing access to those records in their original form (the original bits).[4] Additional services, such as interpreting obsolete data types; providing high-quality, high-performance Web access to rendered records; full-text searching; and finding aids of various kinds, could be provided by NARA as well as others. NARA may decide to provide access itself if no one

---

[4]NARA's activities are for the most part currently limited to a basic preservation task. For paper records, NARA typically provides records in bulk form, and users have the responsibility to sift through the material and select what is appropriate. Similarly, NARA does not provide photocopying services for paper records, but users can pay a third party to do this. In any case, people's expectations for services for digital records will be shaped by their experiences with other online services. Partnerships with others provide one avenue for meeting some of these expectations while concentrating on the central preservation mission.

else does, but NARA has much to gain from partnering with others to provide these services. For example, if in the future common access techniques evolve for digital libraries (together with software to implement them), NARA's ERA can serve as one of the accessible libraries. In cases where there is an identifiable commercial market for the information, third-party commercial organizations might also play a role in providing these additional services.

4. *Consider how to integrate electronic and traditional, nondigital records.* What should be the relationship between electronic records and records in other formats? It was unclear to the committee whether NARA proposes a unified approach for access to all records or whether it develops specific access systems for particular formats of records (e.g. paper, film, photographs, maps, electronic records). This decision will influence the development of finding aids, metadata standards, and search capabilities in the ERA. If multiple format-specific access systems are part of NARA's plan, then the ERA would, for example, need a capability for managing references between the electronic records and records in other formats and for providing facilities for searching across the systems. To minimize complexity and dependency on other systems, it is probably inadvisable to try to integrate access across electronic records and traditional formats in early iterations of the ERA. However, systems should be designed with an eye toward the future integration of traditional and electronic records. For example, it is desirable to assign unique identifiers to both electronic and traditional records to help unify the totality of the archives for researchers.

5. *Consider future interoperation with other repositories.* NARA should also bear in mind the need for interoperability between the ERA and digital repositories in other archives and research libraries.

6. *Consider what can be automated.* Although all the details of work flow and task scheduling need not be specified in detail at the outset, even the initial design must be cognizant of which tasks can and will be carried out manually and which can be automated. The degree of automation will have significant implications for the costs of operating the system. It will also affect NARA's internal business processes, the number and types of staff required (archival vs. technical, professional vs. clerical), and NARA's relationships with other federal agencies. (Detailed discussion of this issue is deferred to the committee's second report.)

All of these considerations imply setting appropriate expectations for the ERA. An archive accessible to the public, in which every record can be presented through a Web browser (or whatever is the preferred public access technique of the day) within a few seconds of a request, could not be deployed today. However, critical ingest, storage, and access capabilities can and should be developed and deployed in pilot programs, and additional capabilities added over time.

SUPPORTING FUTURE ARCHIVISTS AND RESEARCHERS

Future archivists and researchers will be skilled in computing and have better tools and methods than are available today, and thus will be able to manipulate and interpret digital records. Today's researchers are increasingly savvy about analyzing digital records, such as census files, economic data, electronic mail series, and so on. They work from the digital records, not paper copies or other visual presentations of records. Researchers' tools are constantly improving: Techniques for automatically extracting information from text, for summarizing text passages, or for finding complex relationships among several documents have been the subject of research and are becoming commercial products. Also, the digital archivist will be increasingly equipped to examine large quantities of records or collections and to build new catalogs and finding aids that depend on the underlying digital archive. Presentation, conversion, and emulation software of varying capabilities exist as commercial products today.[5] Future users will also have available computers that are far more powerful than today's. Just as NARA will evolve with respect to skills and technologies to handle digital records, so too will researchers and many other customers of the archive.

While the public may want records presented visually on their screens, some members of the research community and digital archivists will desire access to the original bits and associated documentation. They may, for example, wish to verify the accuracy of preferred derived forms or the results obtained through migration or emulation. To support the researcher of the future, the ERA should strive to save the information that will be essential to future reverse engineers: software operating manuals, documentation on data types, and source code when it's available.[6] In some cases, it will also be useful to save executable code associated with the record, to be available for future emulation. It is also important to save information about the processes NARA uses to ingest records (including the source code for the software) so that future researchers can determine exactly how records were processed as they were archived. The ERA should also be alert to new information becoming available—e.g., when a proprietary data type is made public, its specification should be entered into the archive. In short, use the archive to store all technical data about the archive itself.

PRAGMATIC STEPS TO FACILITATE FUTURE ACCESS TO RECORDS

Although it may be the dream of every archivist to make records easily and immediately accessible, a more important objective is to preserve all the information necessary to allow today's bits to be interpreted correctly far in the future. NARA does not have to anticipate or invest in all of the higher-level capabilities that future users might want. As discussed in the previous section, future researchers will have access to tools and expertise that will allow them to manipulate and interpret records. Also, many institutions share an interest with NARA in building tools that support conversion, migration, and emulation, and this technology base will be available to NARA and its users.

However, certain fundamental information about a record is required to support future access. A pragmatic strategy to facilitate future access would include the following elements:

---

[5]One such effort to capture these tools systematically is the PRONOM system being developed by the Public Record Office, the national archives of England and Wales. This capability alone does not necessarily help with obsolescence—i.e., when the last piece of useful software that supports a file format can no longer be executed, the file format becomes unreadable. This need not ever happen, because a software emulator of the bare hardware can later simulate the execution of the application on the digital record. This is the emulation approach to obsolescence.

[6]Even though some of this information may be copyrighted, NARA should make every effort to preserve it—perhaps based on fair use arguments—because it is essential for the future operation of the archive.

1. *Save the original bits.* As is generally appreciated, it is essential that the record be saved in its original form—the original bits—even if the ERA is unable to decode, render, or execute those bits at the time the record is ingested.[7] As the archived data are refreshed onto new media over time, the physical recording of the bits will change; but the ERA will, of course, always be able to deliver the "original bit stream"—the digital data that were ingested. Saving the original bit stream alone is not a guarantee of future access, but it is the foundation on which future preservation measures depend.

2. *Save records in "preferred derived forms" in addition to the original bits.* In many cases it is advisable to save derived forms of the record as well in order to facilitate various forms of access. For example, anticipating a need to make visual presentations of a record, it might be advantageous to prepare, at ingest, a PDF version of a word-processing document; then an access module need only know how to render PDF files rather than how to decode each word-processor data type used for the original records. As another example, anticipating a need to perform full-text searches of records, ingest processing might extract and save an ASCII text file. In some cases, a single derived form might serve both purposes—e.g., an XML encoding of a word-processor document, together with a style sheet,[8] will simplify presentation as well as searching. Also, much like the Rosetta stone, a derived form is an aid to future researchers seeking to interpret the original bit streams.

Although derived forms can be added to the archive long after a record is ingested, it is advisable to create the preferred derived forms as early as possible: The software for preparing such forms may be available at ingest time but may not be readily available years later when a record is accessed. Current record scheduling procedures used by NARA tend to delay ingestion until many years after the records are created. If this gap were shortened, problems of obsolete hardware and software at the time of ingest would be reduced.

Derived forms are, of course, no substitute for retaining and providing access to the original bit stream. A derived form may introduce distortions or errors into the original, or it may omit useful information from the original—e.g., rendering a document may suppress a change history recorded by the word processor in the original data type. Software that creates derived forms may have bugs that introduce errors.

---

[7]The merits of saving original bits for records that were converted during ingestion to the National Archives are illustrated by the case of the NIPS files, which recorded detailed information about Department of Defense (DOD) activities during the Vietnam War. Records in this format, formally known as the National Military Command System 360 Formatted File System, could only be read and interpreted by software developed in the early 1960s for DOD. Later, the DOD withdrew support of the NIPS software, which had the practical effect of making the NIPS format obsolete. When the files were transferred to NARS around 1977-1978, they were decoded and reformatted ("de-NIPSed") to make the records software independent. In the late 1990s it was learned that this decoding, which was done around 1977-1980, had introduced data anomalies in some files. Fortunately, the original NIPS files had been retained and periodically transferred to new storage media at least two times over two decades. Thus, when the data anomalies were discovered, the original NIPS-encoded files could be accessed to correct the anomalies.

[8]Although style sheets are problematical for long-term preservation (for example, they refer to an underlying rendering model that may change with time; see Chapter 3), it is reasonable to use them in conjunction with preferred derived forms, for which it is acceptable to have shorter lifetimes and less than perfect rendering.

3. Be neutral with respect to migration, emulation, or other approaches. There is much debate today in the archival community concerning access to obsolete data types—those for which widely available software and/or hardware is no longer available. One approach is migration: to convert records expressed in expiring data types into modern data types, repeating as those data types in turn expire. An alternative is emulation: Save the original executable software used to manipulate each data type (applications and possibly supporting elements such as the operating system) and emulate the operations of the obsolete computer and thus emulate the old application on a new hardware and software platform.[9] The emulation approach would, of course, also apply where the records themselves consist of executable code.

Migration and emulation have disadvantages as well as advantages. There are other possible preservation approaches as well.[10] None of these approaches has emerged as accepted practice—debate, experiments, and developments will continue.[11]

NARA's most prudent strategy is to use archival procedures that will accommodate both emulation and migration. Both depend on saving the data files in their original data type. Both depend on saving additional information to be able to interpret the bits in the future. NARA should be saving information that will support both migration and emulation in the future.

4. Do not rely primarily on a strategy of converting records to platform- and vendor-independent archiving formats to avoid obsolescence. Conversion of each data type to a platform- and vendor-neutral data type at ingest is a form of migration, with all of its limitations. Such data types cannot, therefore, replace the role of the original data type because they cannot encode all of the elements of all data types.

XML formats are often proposed for this role. It is important to realize that conversion to XML has the same limitations as conversion to other platform- and vendor-independent formats. Sometimes lossless derived types (i.e., where there is an inverse transformation between, for example, a native format and XML) are available; however, one still has to worry about bugs in the transformation software. Box 4.1 discusses XML as a preservation format in more detail. An XML (or other format) derived form may, however, be a very useful adjunct to saving the original data type, as discussed above.

5. Save ephemeral (nonderivable) metadata. Good archival practice is to save as much metadata as possible about each record (and the collection or group in which it resides). As is the case with paper records, the most important metadata to save are the metadata that would otherwise be lost. By contrast, a great deal of metadata can be recovered from the record itself (assuming it can be interpreted). Electronic records lend themselves to automated tools for extracting derivable metadata.

---

[9]See, e.g., Jeff Rothenberg, 1998, *Avoiding Technological Quicksand: Finding a Viable Technical Foundation for Digital Preservation*, Council on Library and Information Resources, Washington, D.C. Available online at <http://www.clir.org/pubs/reports/rothenberg/contents.html>.

[10]Raymond A. Lorie. 2001. "A Project on Preservation of Digital Data." *RLG DigiNews*, 5(3). Available online at <http://www.rlg.org/preserv/diginews/diginews5-3.html>.

[11]This report does not attempt to review the approaches in any detail or evaluate them, though the second report may do so.

BOX 4.1
The Role of XML in Preservation

XML is increasingly proposed as the representation of choice for the long-term preservation of electronic records. XML is a powerful tool and does have a role to play in digital archiving. In particular, it allows the expression of document content separate from presentation, in a nonproprietary, platform-independent manner. Moreover, XML is establishing itself as a widely used tool. However, it is not a panacea for preservation. Here is a brief outline of why it is not:

- *XML is an appealing way to embed markup within text but it is not a self-contained document format.* Even relatively straightforward uses of XML require the use of a set of additional conventions. In particular, XML requires additional support to specify document appearance and does not deal with nontextual or dynamic data. Some of these limitations are being addressed by continual development of XML-related conventions to include style languages and graphics languages and so forth and by embracing other conventions, such as those separately developed for image and multimedia data. Thus representing a document in its entirety requires components using these conventions, and interpreting and rendering an XML document in the future will require recourse to a number of conventions besides XML per se, each of whose proper interpretation would need to be preserved as well. Ensuring the faithful interpretation of these conventions in the future may be a smaller preservation problem than that of ensuring the faithful interpretation of individual document formats, but it is still a preservation problem.
- *XML conveys structure, but not meaning.* XML provides a means of structuring data and allows for the expression of a vocabulary to describe data components of document classes. It does not in itself serve to record what the data mean. Some text tagged as <TITLE> may be the title of the document, or it may be the title of a person ("Herr Doktor Professor"), or it may have neither meaning. Other documents might use <TI> or even <T> to tag their titles. Tags don't convey meaning. A particular markup tag may have meaning specific to the application that created the document and may not be completely captured by XML or other conventions. Even if one retains possession of the schema or Document Type Definition (DTD) used to create the document, one could not reconstruct the document's behavior in its entirely without somehow recording the application-specific semantics of tags. In such cases, conversion to XML has not eliminated the difficult preservation problem of interpreting a document in the future.
- *Conversion to XML is potentially lossy.* Converting a document to XML will inevitably lose information unless the set of XML-related conventions has provision for every feature required by the original document. As the point above suggests, this is not likely to be the case for application-specific semantics. In addition, conversion to XML is a migration, with all the intrinsic risks of approximations, inaccuracies, and errors. XML cannot, therefore, be considered as an alternative to saving the original data objects in their original data types.
- *The set of XML-related conventions comprises components that are new, relatively untested, and not widely supported.* XML itself is 5 years old; many of the related standards are only now coming into being. Even if XML itself remains unchanged forever, these supporting conventions may change considerably or may fail to find widespread support and be replaced by alternative approaches.[1] Thus, using XML may not provide an eternal representation whose bits only need to be made durable but may, rather, require migration or emulation of components.

---

[1]Indeed, DTDs are now being replaced by schemas (XSchema) as a means for specifying the required structure of XML documents.

Consider, by way of example, a memo in the form of a word-processor file obtained from a disk of a White House staffer; the text of the memo identifies the author, the date it was written, and the recipient. The items in the text could be recorded as metadata in anticipation of indexing and searching metadata to find all documents written by a given author, for example. If these metadata are not recorded as the record is ingested, they can be recorded later. By contrast, there are ephemeral metadata about the record—items such as which staffer's PC contained the disk, the date and time the file was written onto the disk, the version of the operating system used—that are not evident from the record itself and that will be lost unless explicitly recorded during ingest.

Databases offer another example. One of the challenges of preserving older databases is that schema documentation is absent. In particular, many critical integrity assumptions are not made explicit, nor can they be deduced by inspecting the data, though in many cases it may be possible to deduce them by analyzing a corpus of queries. Metadata that should be saved would include formal and informal information on schema information, query libraries, and so forth.

6. Save essential external references that are implicit or explicit in the record. As is well-known to archivists, a digital resource will often make references to other resources. In some cases, this is because these resources represent other components of the same "compound document." For example, the image components of some document types are stored as physically separate resources. In general, digital records may comprise multiple explicit components, so to preserve such a record, one must be vigilant about archiving all of its components. Implicit references to resources such as default style sheets or fonts must also be considered. It may be valuable to have a tool or process to ensure that records are in fact saved in their entirety.[12]

In principle, this is a straightforward goal, but no clear solutions exist for managing external references; it is an active area of research in the digital library community. Digital records present some other challenging problems, including these: (1) The cross-references are buried inside the representation rather than being explicitly visible, as are the citations in a paper report, and (2) digital cross-references often use naming schemes (for example, file numbers, local file names, or URLs) that are unstable, not standardized, and may not survive very long. Indeed they may have stopped working by the time that the document is ingested.

---

[12]One way to do this is to simulate, at ingest time, access and presentation of the record, making sure that all resources used by the access and presentation processes are available in the archive. The full set of external references required to support the emulation approach includes the files required to install the application, operating system, and other supporting facilities on bare hardware. These are all implicit external references that would need to be preserved in a software repository, perhaps as part of the ERA or perhaps shared with other digital archives.

The Vesta research project (Allan Heydon et al., 2002, *The Vesta Software Configuration Management System*, SRC Research Report 177, Compaq's Systems Research Center, Palo Alto, Calif. Available online at <http://gatekeeper.dec.com/pub/DEC/SRC/research-reports/abstracts/src-rr-177.html>) developed this sort of capability for all of the code and other resources required to build a large software system.

5

Key Technical Issues

DATA MODEL

Which information and metadata are saved for each preserved record? How are they represented? Using which data types? The "data model" is the specification that answers these questions. The ingest process builds representations of records that conform to the model and the access process finds records, deciphers the representation according to the model, and presents the results to the user. The data model is thus a key interface in the system: it is the interface between the ingest process and the access process, using a linkage provided by the storage system. It is an "interface to the future."[1]

The data model must be designed to evolve, because new data types and requirements will emerge over the life of the system. Thus a careful design for the data model that tries to anticipate future ERA needs will simplify the system. While it is easy to allow different models to coexist in a single archive simply by labeling each record with the identity of the data model used to store it, a proliferation of data models will result in a costly proliferation of software to interpret them.

This chapter highlights some of the properties of a data model, principally to tie it into discussion elsewhere in the section. Box 5.1 shows some possible elements of a digital record. Many variations are possible; for example, the metadata for each file (original and derived) might be recorded separately, with the metadata that pertain to the record as a whole kept in

---

[1] Although this expression may seem trite, it accurately describes the vital role of the data model. The ingest process must prepare a digital representation of the record that supports future access processes—some of which may not be created until years after the ingestion of the record. Thus, the interface must be designed to ignore the inner workings of access modules. At the same time, the properties of the interface will enable or constrain what future access modules can do with the record.

> **BOX 5.1**
> **Some Possible Elements of a Digital Record**
>
> 1. *Original files:* one or more digital files, the original bit stream or native form of the record represented in its native data type. A record may consist of more than one file, e.g., a report in which each chapter is represented by a separate word-processor file.
>
> 2. *Optional derived forms: digital files obtained from the original files by a converter.* ERA policies might encourage certain kinds of derived forms to be saved, for example these:
> —A form whose data type is chosen to simplify "presentation" or "rendering" the record into a visible form for printing or display.
> —A form whose data type is chosen to simplify content searching.
>
> 3. *Metadata for the record.* In addition to the usual metadata normally captured for records, there is additional metadata associated with electronic records, such as:
> —Data types of the digital files and derived forms, with sufficient information to allow finding documentation about the data types. Data types will usually be versioned.
> —Relationship among the digital files that constitute the record.
> —Integrity checks—e.g., a cryptographic hash, for the digital files and the metadata.
> —Ephemeral/nonderivable metadata—i.e., properties of the context in which the record was created that are not specified in the record itself.
> —Derived metadata—i.e., properties that have been extracted from the record.
> —Provenance and history, such as evidence that it was transferred accurately to the archive (a form of ephemeral metadata). In the case of derived forms, metadata identify the converter used to obtain the derived form from the original.
> —Unique identifier of the record.
> —The data type of the metadata—i.e., the definitions of metadata elements used to construct the metadata for this record.

a separate file. Metadata that pertain to collections as a whole might be stored in yet another file, referenced in metadata for each record in the collection.

The data model must also deal with embedding and aggregation. Embedding occurs when one record is embedded within another, e.g., a spreadsheet is embedded as an attachment within an e-mail message. Aggregation occurs when several records are saved together, e.g., a series of e-mail messages is saved in a single file, even though each message is to be treated as a separate record. Another form of aggregation that may be desirable is the container—e.g., as used by the SDSC demonstration—which simply collects a group of records into a single digital file for more efficient handling by the file system.[2]

The archive should contain complete documentation about all versions of the data model, including specifications of the data types it uses. Since metadata sets are likely to proliferate

---

[2]A container is distinct from an archivist's "collection." A collection may span several containers, and several collections might fit within a single container.

and be complex, it is essential that any use of metadata be linked to a complete definition of its terms.

Several aspects of the data model require more discussion:

- *Evolution.* The key to smooth evolution of the data model is to carefully label each digital file that is part of the stored record with its type; when the file is read, the type identifier selects software that can interpret the file correctly. This is sometimes called "self-identifying data." Whenever a data type is chosen as part of the data model, the system designer should ask, How do I introduce a new version of this data type without disrupting existing records? Clearly, if new types are introduced too frequently, the proliferation of types will lead to overly complex software to decode them all. Note that types must be versioned—it is not enough to say "this is a Microsoft Word document." A version number and perhaps platform (e.g., PC or Macintosh) are required for unambiguous identification.
- *Unique identifier.* The ERA should assign to each record a unique identifier that can be used, both inside and outside the archive, to refer to records. Such identifiers are used inside a system to identify records without regard to their location or storage mechanism; they are used outside a system to specify a link to a specific record. A related question is how separate parts of the representation of a record (e.g., distinct original files or derived forms) are identified. The unique identifier for digital records should be harmonized with ways of identifying other records held by NARA.[3] There are a number of digital identifier techniques and implementations today, and it is entirely possible that the particular scheme used by the ERA may change a few times over the lifetime of the archive. The system design should accommodate such changes.
- *Modifying the archive.* Although the principal idea of an archive is that records, once ingested, must not be modified, the ERA must allow certain kinds of information to be added or changed. Records themselves, once ingested, are rarely, if ever, modified or removed. It may be advantageous to add new derived forms long after the record was first ingested, perhaps when improved migration tools and techniques become available. And some of the metadata surrounding records (such as conditions of use, where to find derived versions, and relation to records added at a later date) may need to be modified. Some metadata may need to be updated—for example, to record ephemeral metadata that come to light after the original ingestion, or to note changes to access controls for a record that result from new regulations or the passage of time. Importantly, all such modifications need to be logged in such a way that it is possible later to identify causes of mistakes and untangle them. It also may be wise to design the system so that information cannot be deleted, only augmented.[4]

---

[3]NARA does have a procedure for establishing a unique identifier for each record series for its paper records. Essentially, the records hierarchy has 13 levels, from Record Group to item, that assign a unique identifier based on the specific Record Group and the level of the record. This does not go all the way down to a unique ID for each record. It would be possible to add additional data (such as a date and sequence number) to provide unique identification.

[4]Computer science researchers have designed "write-once" file systems in which it is not possible to delete a file, only to add new files or supplant old ones (add new versions of old files). This may not be a wise approach for the ERA. Suppose, however, certain records must be expunged from the archive, perhaps as a result of a court order. Even though rare, such a modification might be required.

• *Commonalities with digital libraries.* The issues confronting the design of a data model for the ERA are almost exactly the same as those for a digital library. Unfortunately, there are no standard data models that can simply be adopted by NARA. Nevertheless, NARA should seek to align its design with that of digital libraries, since this will increase the likelihood of providing uniform access to libraries and archives in the future.

Closely related to the specification of the data model is a set of policies used to operate the archive. For example, the data model determines how derived forms are recorded in the archive, but a policy will specify which kinds of derived forms should be generated for a collection, perhaps specified as part of the collection's profile. Policies will also apply to modifications to the archive—who may introduce modifications and under what conditions (perhaps even requiring two staffers to confirm certain kinds of changes, as is common practice in the financial services industry).

Data Types and Obsolescence

The data model confronts the most challenging problem of an archive: For records to be useful many decades after they are ingested, they must be expressed in the data model using data types that can still be decoded and interpreted at the time of access. By that time the computers and software used to create the original records may be obsolete.

The archival community has written at length on this topic.[5] The debate over emulation vis-à-vis migration continues (see the brief discussion of emulation and migration in the preceding chapter), and neither one is firmly established as the only way to preserve digital records. In fact, some researchers in digital preservation reject the notion that emulation and migration are mutually exclusive (assuming, as we do here, that the requisite information to support each is retained) and argue that each is appropriate under particular circumstances. Consequently, the ERA should be designed to:

• Record in the archive the information necessary to support both emulation and migration when and if either becomes common. The original bit stream and careful records of the software environment in which it was created (data type and ephemeral metadata to record the fonts, operating system, application program, and other digital resources or pointers to them) are essential.

• Function adequately in the absence of either emulation or migration solutions. This requires some pragmatic choices, which are discussed here and in Chapter 4.

NARA shares with others an interest in making one or another of these preservation strategies operational, such as building emulators for a few of the most popular computers.

---

[5]See, for example, Jeff Rothenberg, 1995 (revised in 1999), "Ensuring the Longevity of Digital Documents," *Scientific American* 272(1): 42-47; revised and expanded version available online at <http://www.clir.org/pubs/archives/ensuring.pdf>; Task Force on Archiving Digital Information, 1996, *Preserving Digital Information* (commissioned by the Commission on Preservation and Access and the Research Libraries Group, Inc. [RLG]), Mountain View, Calif., RLG, available online at <http://www.rlg.org/ArchTF/tfadi.index.htm>; and Howard Besser, 2000, "Digital Longevity," in *Handbook for Digital Projects: A Management Tool for Preservation and Access*, Maxine Sitts, ed. Andover, Mass., Northeast Document Conservation Center, pp. 155-166. See also Stephen Manes, 1998, "Time and Technology Threaten Digital Archives . . .," *New York Times*, April 7, p. F4.

KEY TECHNICAL ISSUES

This option is worthy of further exploration. However, as a future option rather than a present reality, the ERA program cannot depend on a particular preservation strategy at present.

The preceding chapter describes a pragmatic approach to making records useful in the future: Anticipate common purposes to which records may be put in the future (e.g., display or text searching) and prepare, as each record is ingested, one or more derived forms of the record, chosen to streamline future access for those uses. As a complement to possible future efforts that provide access through such techniques as emulation or migration, the pragmatic strategy is to support access by using a smaller number of data types to express the derived forms of records. These are referred to in this report as "preferred data types."

This approach requires characterizing the most common (future) uses of different kinds of records and choosing associated preferred data types for the derived forms.[6] These choices, and the kinds of access users seek, may, of course, change over time in ways not anticipated today—but some reasonable projections of use that address likely forms of access can be made.

As an illustration, here are some common uses of records and possible choices for preferred data types to support the use:

- *Presentation of a document in visual form (printed or displayed).* Some preferred data types: image data types (fax, TIFF), Portable Document Format (PDF), ASCII text, XML-encoded document with a style sheet that specifies rendering parameters.[7]
- *Searching the text of many documents.* Some preferred data types: PDF,[8] ASCII text, and XML-encoded document.
- *Loading a relational table into a database.* Some preferred data types: comma-separated variables (CSV), dBase, XML encoding.

The derived forms may fail to reveal one or more properties of the original record but nevertheless will make the record accessible many years after its ingest. For example, a presentation created from an XML-encoded derived form may not break lines and pages in the same places as the original word-processing software; a PDF file derived from a word-processor file will not retain the change history recorded in the native data type. But supporting PDF as a presentation data type is far easier than supporting the very large number of data types from which PDF files can be derived.

The choice of preferred data type will require consideration of the loss of fidelity compared with the native form.[9] A future researcher considering the use of a derived form will need this information to determine whether to be satisfied with a derived form or to take extra steps to interpret the native data type.

Retaining one or more derived forms will add somewhat to the storage requirements of the archive, but wise choices of preferred data types will probably not increase storage require-

---

[6]It is important to note that manipulating (editing or changing) a preserved record is not a common use, so preferred data types can have much more constrained aims than native data types.

[7]Box 4.1 discusses some of the limitations associated with XML encoding.

[8]Most PDF writers create files that are easy to search for text strings. However, it is certainly possible to create PDF files that defy simple searching.

[9]For some records, it may be difficult to carefully enumerate and document this loss. The cost and limitations of this evaluation should be factored into the decision to create preferred data types.

ments by more than a factor of 2. In many cases, a single derived form can serve all the common uses anticipated for the record. In some cases, the native data type may itself be a preferred data type that satisfies all the anticipated uses.

The reason for recording derived forms when the record is ingested is simple: It is at this time that software to create the derived forms is most likely to be available. Unfortunately, the ingest process often occurs many years after a record was originally created, by which time the software to create derived forms may already be obsolete. Then the process may require custom software or may be very difficult (e.g., if the native data type remained proprietary and fell into disuse).

If the derived forms of a record are to be useful decades after they are created, the preferred data types must be chosen carefully. NARA will need to select and extend the collection of preferred data types. Preferred data types would have at least some of the following properties:

- *In common use.* The data type should be in common use and reasonably expected to remain so for some time. NARA should not have to make decisions about common data types quickly, so the list can evolve slowly as NARA watches for common forms.[10]
- *Well documented.* The data type should have sufficient documentation to allow modestly skilled programmers to write software to process the data type for its intended uses, such as presentation. Standards are usually well documented, but often proprietary data types also have fine documentation (e.g., PDF[11] and RTF[12] today) and may be reasonable candidates for data types of derived forms. Many proprietary data types also have corresponding "external" or "interchange" data types that are candidates for preferred data types. It is an added benefit if the data type is simple.
- *Slowly changing.* If the definition of the data type is stable, the cost of supporting it is reduced.
- *Free from intellectual property encumbrances.* It is a disadvantage if processing a data type requires licenses from intellectual property owners. (In the long run, NARA may wish to seek agreements that processing archival documents represents "fair use" of such property, or seek specific legislative relief.) NARA—or the federal government—may wish to induce vendors to transfer obsolete data type specifications to the public domain.
- *Software available in the public domain or in open-source form.* For each preferred data type, NARA will need to obtain and maintain associated access software. In many cases, NARA can take advantage of software written by others. Note, however, that to be useful to NARA the software must be in a form that is likely to be useful decades from now—for example, that can be ported as needed to new hardware and software platforms.

Choices of preferred data types for the ERA should also be influenced by common practice

---

[10]If preferred data types are chosen carefully, it is possible that the period of time before a preferred data type must be decommissioned may be lengthened considerably.

[11]Adobe Systems' "Portable Document Format," <http://partners.adobe.com:80/asn/developer/acrosdk/docs/filefmtspecs/PDFReference.pdf>.

[12]Microsoft's Rich Text Format, <http://msdn.microsoft.com/library/en-us/dnrtfspec/html/rtfspec.asp>.

in digital libraries, other digital archives, and mainstream computing.[13] Common choices would lead to opportunities for sharing access software among such partners and may increase the likelihood of commercial products that will reduce the cost of developing or evolving the ERA. Selecting a relatively small number of preferred data types has the additional advantage of allowing NARA staff to become truly expert in the technical aspects of particular formats.

Derived forms can also be used to address other needs of the ERA. For example, a database in which some fields are public and others have special access restrictions might have a derived form for public access, with sensitive fields omitted. Redacted versions of a record might be stored as derived forms with relaxed access controls.

Derived forms may also be a simple way to deal with unique or complex data types. For example, an archivist seeking to preserve records stored in a unique IT system with unknown internal data structures might run a collection of "reports"—text files intended for printing—which taken together reveal all the information retained in the unknown data structures. Archiving these reports as derived forms might be the most practical approach to preserving the essential contents of a record.

Metadata

Metadata are conventionally expressed as a series of "attribute, value" pairs (also sometimes called "tag, value" pairs). A metadata set is a collection of attribute names and corresponding definitions used to express metadata. There are no standard universal metadata sets, though many popular subsets exist (e.g., Dublin Core[14]). Some attempts are under way to try to relate all metadata definitions to a common ontology, but this complex approach is very risky. It seems clear that metadata sets will change frequently over the lifetime of the ERA and that the system should be designed to accommodate such change, an observation confirmed by the experience of the SDSC demonstrations. XML offers one convenient syntax today for recording metadata, in part because it is easily extensible; it is already the representation of choice in the digital library community.

For metadata saved in the ERA to be useful, users must be able to obtain precise definitions of metadata tags. It is for this reason that each metadata record should identify the metadata set it uses and provide a way to find, in the archive itself, the definitions of the tags in that set. As discussed in Chapter 3, the SDSC work showed that indexing pertinent metadata in a relational database offers a surprisingly simple and effective way to find archived records.

Some metadata saved in the ERA must be interpreted by the ERA software itself, e.g., tags that specify data types of the digital files that constitute the record. In order to accommodate changing metadata sets without enshrining specific metadata tag names throughout the software, some form of lookup should be used to convert from the tag name used in the specific metadata set to a name that is meaningful only to the software.

---

[13]Preferred data types have been selected in a number of programs. For example, the DSpace project (<www.dspace.org>) provides varying levels of support for different formats. The Federal Court system's Case Management/Electronic Case Filing (CM/ECF) system, which allows courts to accept filings and provides access to filed documents over the Internet, has adopted the PDF format. For more information on the CM/ECF system, see <http://pacer.psc.uscourts.gov/cmecf/> and <http://pacer.psc.uscourts.gov/documents/press.pdf>.

[14]<http://dublincore.org>

STORAGE

The storage function of the ERA is used to save files for a long time (perhaps it should be called a "long-term file system"[15]). It thus serves as a transparent bridge between ingest and access functions: The files produced by ingest are delivered without modification to access. In many respects it is like any other file system. Some of its requirements, though not commonplace, are shared with other very large, mission-critical systems, including these:

- *Scalability.* It must be able to grow to hold many (even hundreds of) petabytes of data, in many billions or even trillions of individual files.
- *Robustness.* It must not corrupt data or fail to deliver data requested.
- *Access control.* Only authorized software, under the control of authorized staff, may store files or make other modifications to what is stored.

It is in the area of robustness over a very long period of time—the lifetime of its data is longer than that of any known data storage device or medium—that the system presents unusual requirements.[16]

The following strategies can be used to preserve digital files for many decades:

- *Store redundant replicas.* To survive the failure of a storage device, information is stored redundantly. But care must be taken to categorize failure modes and determine appropriate storage strategies. For example, if a file is stored on two different disks, both of which are located in the same room, a fire might destroy both copies. So some kind of geographic replication is a must—usually achieved today by saving copies of a file at one or more remote sites connected by a high-speed network. Replication is governed by policies enforced by the file system that specify how many copies should be kept, where they should be stored, and so on.
- *Detect errors and correct them automatically.* In order to detect failed devices in a large file system, it is necessary to use a background task to read all the data in the system constantly and check for errors caused by deterioration. This process requires computing a hash or checksum of each file and comparing the value with a value computed from the same data when it was first stored.[17] When a corrupted file is detected, one of its redundant copies is used to create a fresh copy somewhere else so as to conform to the replication policy. (And other files stored on the same device that produced errors are probably also moved, since the device as a whole may be failing. The device is then removed from service or replaced.)
- *Refresh media.*[18] As storage media age, copy all the files stored on them to new devices,

---

[15]Calling it an archival file system risks confusing it with archival file systems offered by some computer system vendors, often as part of a hierarchical storage management product.

[16]The robustness requirements may well not be uniform for all records. The requirements might, for example, be a property of a record that is assigned at ingest time and might be reflected in how much the storage system "invests" in preserving that record. This is a good example of how complicated some of the architectural issues for the ERA can be.

[17]Disk and tape recording formats include checksums that are verified on each read, but these are viewed as insufficiently robust. A file-level hash is advisable as well.

[18]The term "refresh" is preferred to "migrate," because the second term is used to describe a conversion of data type.

and remove the old devices from service. This step requires that new devices can be attached to the file system at all times over the life of the system.

- *Rebuild directories and indexes by scanning the archive.* If sensitive data that describe the structure of a file system are lost, the entire file system can be scanned to rebuild the data. Such a design requires storing files on the disk in a way that records their structure within the file system.
- *Use implementation diversity.* To guard against losing files because of errors in the file-system software, replicas of a file can be saved in file systems with distinct implementations.

These techniques are all widely used (or at least widely advocated) today. The engineering challenge for NARA is that no one has yet demonstrated that they can, together, implement a file system that will preserve files for a hundred years or more.[19]

The scalability of the file system, as well as its ability to connect new storage devices to replace old ones, can be achieved using network-connected storage systems. When it is no longer possible or economically feasible to expand the capacity of any existing storage system, a new system is procured, attached to the network, and configured to participate in the overall file system.

The overall file system operates as a "federation" of the network-connected storage components. This technique uses a software layer that makes the collection of network-connected systems appear to be a single file system. It would provide services such as these:

- Naming of files, and mapping names to locations where files are stored;
- Routing file access requests to the appropriate network-connected store, incorporating newly added stores, and providing the necessary "drivers" for new classes of network storage services;
- Access control;
- Redundancy control, as described above (maintaining redundant copies, scanning for corrupted files, refreshing old media, removing old storage from service);
- Audit log, used to track all changes to the file system;
- Performance measurement, used to determine the load placed on the file system, its internal overhead (e.g., for integrity auditing or media refresh), occurrences of faulty media, and so on;
- Management processes, used to modify configurations when new storage is added to the federation or to direct that old storage should be evacuated and abandoned, etc.

The software layer insulates the ERA clients of the file system from the various implementations used in the federation. Implementations can be replaced by changing at most a driver in the software. The Storage Request Broker (SRB), used in the SDSC demonstrations, is one example of such a distributed file system, but the technology is quite common.[20]

---

[19]Digital computers and their storage devices were unknown in 1903!

[20]The federated file system model is a mature, well-understood technology. Multiple implementations exist, of which the SRC is only one example. The research community is exploring new technologies for decentralized storage, location, and retrieval of information that may offer additional capabilities in the future. But NARA should focus today on more mature technologies that enjoy commercial support and are likely to be around for a while.

Different storage policies may apply to different parts of the distributed file system. Working storage for both ingest and access modules may be provided by part of the file system federation. Because working storage need not be retained for decades, some of the redundancy, auditing, and media refreshing policies that are required for the long-term storage will not apply to the working stores.

The distributed file system may use COTS products to provide network-connected storage. Note that some of the requirements and policies of the distributed file system interact with properties of the network storage—e.g., a conventional network-accessible file system product will not be able to identify all files that should be moved when a corrupted file is detected. Modern file systems may have redundancy techniques built in (e.g., RAID[21]) that interact with redundancy policies of the federation. These issues will have to be carefully addressed to determine how COTS products can be used in the file system.

Storage must be geographically distributed in order to prevent catastrophic loss of data.[22] One possibility is that remote components are nevertheless managed as part of a single file system. Since one of the key reasons for geographical diversity is to guard against total failure of a site, it will be important that the entire file system can survive loss of a site. Managing replication to avoid single points of failure is one of the jobs of the federation software.

Note that most properties of the file system apply to file systems required for digital libraries. There are opportunities for NARA to collaborate with others to arrive at common specifications and implementations. The file system should be designed without knowledge of the data model, so the file system implementation can be shared even if the data model is not.

File System Performance Requirements

The file system must be designed to meet the scale and performance requirements that the ERA will face. Examples of some of the file-system-specific performance metrics required to guide design are these:

- *Size*. What is the target size of the initial repository? How many bytes? How many files? How will each of these scale over time?
- *Bandwidth*. How much bandwidth will be necessary to support ingest, access, file scanning, and media refresh?
- *Refresh time*. How long will it take to copy or recreate the entire archive? This parameter is important, because if the file system becomes so large that it takes 5 years to copy and the refresh cycle needs to be repeated every 4 years, the design will not work.
- *Ingest rate*. At what rate will new records be incorporated into the repository? Note that the geographic redundancy requirement means that the ingest rate heavily influences the bandwidth required for communication with remote storage, as new data are copied to remote sites.

---

[21]The acronym originally referred to "redundant array of inexpensive disks," but today it commonly refers to "redundant array of independent disks."

[22]The only other alternative is to make backup tapes and carry them far offsite. Although tape backup is simpler than a hierarchical storage management system using tape, a remote file system is even simpler because it avoids tapes altogether.

KEY TECHNICAL ISSUES 45

• *Response time.* Must the system support real-time queries? If so, what are reasonable response time targets?
• *Life span.* At what rate are components expected to be replaced (particularly the storage devices themselves). What is the unit of replacement? What is the impact of replacement on performance?

Performance requirements for access are harder to anticipate than those for ingest and storage. Although the conventional model for access is a user conducting a search and reading records on a computer screen, it is also likely that users in the future will want to run statistical queries, perform data mining and automated cross-referencing and correlation, and do other things that a future access system may or may not support and which could have significant bearing on an access system's performance requirements. Moreover, it is likely that access will involve creating full-text indexes of collections, which imposes an additional load on the long-term file system.

These targets may eliminate certain technology choices (for example, access performance requirements might eliminate the possibility that tape could be used as a primary preservation medium). They are essential to guide the implementation of software that controls the federation—for example, the design of the naming system is quite sensitive to anticipated system size.

Selecting Storage Media

Presently, NARA stores most of its electronic records using off-line tape storage; this is also the approach used in the SDSC demonstrations. For new systems, disks are becoming the preferred storage choice. Instead of storing files on tape and copying and storing backups offsite, digital archives are kept on geographically separated disk replicas. Data are transferred to other locations using either a network connection or by shipping disks or servers containing the files offsite. While other storage media, such as optical disks, have been considered for long-term preservation, they suffer from many of the same drawbacks as tape.

Disks have a number of advantages compared with tape, including these:

• *Lower cost.* The overall system costs of tape and disk storage are roughly equal, but the cost per byte of disk storage is declining faster than that of tape. (Cost comparisons of disk and tape are complicated by debates about what to count, especially the human support staff required.) Projections favor disks in coming years.
• *Volumetric density.* Disks take less physical space to store the same amount of data. Densities are improving by a factor of about 2 every year.
• *Fast access.* Disks allow fast access, suitable for interactive applications. By contrast, tape processing incurs a variety of access delays. Tapes must be mounted (either by a robot or manually) and once mounted, must be read sequentially.
• *Less complexity.* Disk-only file systems are much simpler than hierarchical storage management schemes that must manage the migration of data between disk and tape. Tapes also require large file sizes to be efficient, which results in complex file-aggregation mechanisms. If accessing a record requires reading files from several disks or tapes because they were created at different times (e.g., metadata or derived forms that were added long after the record was ingested), disk-only systems will perform far better than tape systems. A tape system could be

designed to collect and rewrite in one spot disparate portions of a record, but this adds complexity.

- *Automatic error detection and recovery.* Regardless of actual disk lifetimes, the file system must be designed to save files on more than one disk and perform file integrity checks frequently enough that files corrupted due to bad disks are identified before the last replica of the file is also unreadable. When a disk is found to be bad, all files stored on it are copied elsewhere and the disk is removed from service or replaced.

There is more to learn about the use of disk storage for long-term preservation. The details of disk drive failure mechanisms and statistics are not yet fully known, because manufacturers are loath to release data. It is not clear, for example, whether disks should be powered down if they are not expected to be used for a while or whether a disk that has been powered off for a long time should be run periodically to lubricate its bearings. There are indications that the lifetime of some disks is somewhat reduced when they are operated near other disks because of coupled vibration.

No choice of storage medium avoids the need for storage refresh. Storage refresh should be anticipated from the outset and embedded in the design and operation of the ERA.

The trends in cost and performance of disks also suggest that a system designed for a lifetime as long as that of the ERA should use disks exclusively. Final decisions about which media to use will require more detailed analysis of costs (initial procurement, ongoing maintenance, and labor), physical space requirements, access times, media degradation rates, data loss rates, integrity requirements, and so forth. The ERA design should, in any case, in no way preclude moving to disk-only storage.

INGEST

Ingest processes are designed according to the data types[23] of incoming records and the work flows of the organization building the archive. Some digital document repositories have been created with a streamlined process for scanning large numbers of uniform paper documents or ingesting particular digital formats and building a repository using very little manual labor. At the other extreme, an archivist presented with hard disks retrieved from the White House computers or a pile of old floppy disks confronts diverse records and unique challenges that may not be easily automated.

The experience of archivists has tended to be ad hoc—activities carried out by skilled IT professionals with a collection of tools for dissecting and processing arcane data types. Some writers envision the ingest process supported by an "accessioning workbench"[24] that suggests

---

[23]Throughout this report, "data type" is used to identify the data-encoding rules whereby various kinds of records (documents, electronic mail messages, pictures, database entires, etc.) are expressed as a collection of bits. Thus an image might be represented by bits whose data type is TIFF or GIF or JPEG or any of a number of other such specifications. "File format" is often used interchangeably with "data type," but "data type" is used exclusively throughout this report because the literal interpretation of "file format" is overly restricted to files of bits. For example, when an image is embedded in an e-mail message that is itself embedded in a "folder" of many messages saved in a file, the bits representing the image cannot properly be called a "file."

[24]Kenneth Thibodeau. 2001. "Building the Archives of the Future," *D-Lib Magazine* 7(2), February. Available online at <http://www.dlib.org/dlib/february01/thibodeau/02thibodeau.html>.

the problem-solving skills and craftsmanship required. NARA will probably need to devise multiple ingest processes and associated software to cope with the variability of records presented to it.

Designing ingest processes depends critically on the kinds and quantities of records to be processed. This is why it is important that NARA inventory digital records waiting to be ingested and survey the records that agencies will soon pass on to NARA.

In the past, a large fraction of the ingest effort has been devoted to dealing with the problems of extracting data from physical media, such as floppy disks of great age that have suffered untold abuses. These media-related problems will subside in the future for several reasons: (1) data are increasingly stored on hard disks, whose reliability and capacity have steadily improved; (2) because a high-speed network interface is standard on computers large and small, moving data to modern media is greatly simplified; and (3) computer owners—and especially professional IT departments—can and commonly do move important data to new media to ensure its continued accessibility. Where records are stored on off-line media such as tape and ingest is deferred for years after record creation, media issues will persist.

Unfortunately, a far more serious and growing problem confronts the digital archivist: a profusion of data types, many of which are very complex. Simply checking that records are represented in their claimed data type can be difficult—it may require running hard-to-find software on rare computer systems. While "data dumps" may have sufficed in the past to distinguish ASCII from EBCDIC databases, checking the integrity of a modern word processing file is much more difficult—it may require running the word processor software that created the record.[25] Moreover, many of these data files may contain hidden references to external data that should be considered for archiving as well.

Another important problem is that of data management—determining which digital files represent records that should be preserved. When many files are saved in an ad hoc fashion on a government computer, such as the personal computer of a White House staffer, and no formal records-management process is used, the files must sifted to find records to archive. For example, NARA was presented with several hundred hard disk drives from the White House containing the digital record of the Clinton administration. Extracting files from these disks was relatively easy, but discarding system files and duplicates recorded on several machines required additional steps.[26]

Although experience offers little advice on general strategies for ingest, the committee offers some suggestions:

- *Try to reduce the variability of records scheduled for preservation.* Identifying preferred data types and encouraging creating agencies to adopt these as native data types is one approach. Advance awareness of new data types being presented to NARA can guide adoption of new preferred derived forms and development of associated software. (The ERA will, of course,

---

[25] It would be useful and relatively easy to save the validation software at ingest time.
[26] Because these files come from the White House, NARA has to also examine each record to determine whether it should be classified as personal, political, or governmental, because the three types of records require different treatment.

still have to be capable of ingesting the full variety of data types used in the federal government, which will roughly correspond to the full variety of data types in use more broadly.)

- *Automate common cases, for example by creating scripts that carry out the transformations and checks required.* For example, since it appears likely that e-mail records (with attachments) will be an increasingly common record form, it makes sense to invest processing as much e-mail as possible automatically.
- *Develop a plan for handling metadata.* Ephemeral metadata must be captured as part of the ingest process. It may also be easy to capture some derived metadata as well and store the results along with the archival record. However, sophisticated metadata extraction, text summarization, and searching need not be part of an initial system. Such processes can be deferred until later generations of the system without losing information, and better technology to automate these processes may be available in the future.
- *Develop explicit work flow designs.* Records may need to be reviewed by an archivist or other non-IT professional in order to make essential dispositions. For example, presidential records need to be categorized as government, political, or personal and handled accordingly. Some records may need to be reviewed for security or other access-control issues and then tagged with suitable access-control metadata. (This work flow requirement has implications for system design; see below.) The need to accommodate diverse work flows may be the most challenging aspect of designing ingest software. Both the work flows and the software must be able to evolve over time.
- *Design work flows, software, and auditing processes so that the integrity of records is guaranteed.* Ideally, the creating agency should be able to certify that the records, as they appear in the archive, are genuine.
- As noted above, *record in the archive the details of processes used to ingest records* so that future researchers are able to understand any processing or translation applied to the records during ingest.

Finally, NARA will need to establish crisp guidelines governing modifications that staff make to records as they are ingested. Vigilant checking for errors or inconsistencies in data might lead to a desire to fix errors or fill in gaps in data. Such actions would not be tolerated for paper records and should not be permitted for digital records. It is thus important to document what actions are taken with respect to media renewal or creating preferred format types. If any changes occur in the underlying bit stream of digital records (without regard to their impact on rendering), the preservation documentation should call attention to this. If data are missing and the agency cannot locate the missing data, then the documentation should call this to the attention of users. Digital records are susceptible to accidental or deliberate alteration; ingest processes should pay attention to end-to-end integrity assurance.

The highly variable nature of ingestion processes will, as noted above, probably result in an evolving set of ad hoc processes and software. However, there are a few system engineering ideas that could be applied to ingestion:

- The ingestion of a set of records (e.g., a collection) by possibly ad hoc processes should create a set of files conforming to the ERA data model stored in such a way that the normal ERA access processes can retrieve them. These files might be considered to be provisionally entered into the archive. They are stored and accessed using the standard file-system interface, but they have yet to be formally released into the archive.[27] In their provisional state, the files can be accessed normally to be checked by the creating agency or the NARA ingestion staff or to be reviewed by an archivist to assign record-specific properties such as access controls. Because the files are provisional, they may be deleted if errors are found. Finally, the provisional files are formally entered into the archive.

- A set of records ready to be entered into the archive (the provisional files above) should be checked for consistency using an automated checker to ensure that they conform to the data model. For example, metadata should be checked to ensure that essential metadata tags are present, that all files are properly described, etc. It may be useful to verify each file using an integrity checker associated with the file's data type. For example, if one of the files is expressed in an XML encoding with an associated data type definition (DTD) or schema, the checker should verify that the XML file conforms to these specifications (i.e., it is a valid XML document). Validation provides an opportunity to identify records that may have been garbled at some stage; marking nonconforming documents allows one to potentially identify problems (e.g., when records are exported from the creating agency) and forestall downstream processing errors.

- Although ingestion software may be ad hoc, there are common modules that should be implemented once and shared, e.g., data-type checkers and converters.

The cost of operating the ERA will depend critically on the amount of manual labor required to staff the ingest process. If significant amounts of metadata must be entered and checked by humans or if digital records arrive at NARA in corrupted or incomplete form, the ingest process will bog down and ultimately limit the ERA's ability to meet its mandate. Providing the right kind of user interfaces or automation for streamlining this process will depend on the details of the human processing required. This is another area where estimates based on records already produced by government agencies are required to design the ERA.

ACCESS

Accessing the ERA should be much like accessing a digital library: It requires a means to find a record, retrieve the record, and possibly convert it into another data type for delivery to the requestor. Digital libraries today routinely deliver their content via Web browsers or download using a number of standard presentation formats. Although these systems are largely custom built, commercial software components are increasingly used.

Perhaps the most vexing problem facing ERA is that the performance required for accessing offerings, especially online access, is unknown. Some collections will be used a great deal; others will not. Moreover, the design and deployment of access software changes as demand changes. Doubtless access modules will need to be redesigned several times as access statistics become known or change.

For collections that are accessed frequently by online users, it will probably be advisable to "stage" the files by copying them from the long-term file system to a separate file system

---

[27]The SDSC demonstrations exploited this idea to great benefit.

designed for high-performance access. As access demand for the collection grows, more access modules can be deployed on available computers, all working from the same set of staged files. The staged files act as a cache of the files held in the long-term file system. (Such staging, by decoupling the archival copy of the record from potentially malicious users, helps protect record integrity.)

Some kinds of access may require preprocessing an entire collection of records (or more). For example, full-text search software usually builds and saves an index to a corpus in order to offer faster searching than would be possible by simply scanning all the contents for each search request. Indexing requires that records be rendered in an appropriate format. Software that summarizes text or automatically extracts metadata (e.g., names of people or businesses cited in news feeds) likewise builds a database of extracted information. Even simple searches based on metadata of collections or records will require building an index.[28] These indexing and access techniques will need to save extracted information temporarily on a separate file system—not part of the long-term file system.[29] While these indexes can be deleted and rebuilt if necessary, dismal performance will result if a large portion of the archive must be scanned in order to rebuild one or more indexes. As a result, techniques are required for storing and updating these files incrementally, as changes are made to the archive.

NARA will need to set expectations for access to ERA records. In preparing this report, the committee has assumed that users will receive either a digital file representing the record (in its native data type or in one of the available derived forms) or will be presented a visual representation of the record. The committee has not addressed the much more difficult problems of presenting online access to software that can manipulate one or more records (or providing access to records that are themselves executable).

By way of example, consider the variety of online access methods offered today by the Census Bureau to the 2000 census data.[30] Some offerings are simple tables, presented visually. Others are responses to trivial queries against an underlying database. Some are sophisticated statistical extraction and calculation applications working from a census database. Which kinds of access could ERA users expect to this data decades hence? Probably the first, and perhaps the second (it's not hard to provide a simple search mechanism for tables). Offering complex applications, however, would not only place a computational burden on the ERA, but also would require emulation, porting, or some other technique to allow today's software to run in the far future. NARA will have to make quality-of-service choices about whether and when to invest in such capabilities. It may be adequate to allow users to simply download all the data and process it themselves. Alternatively, if there is sufficient public demand, the Census Bureau itself might take on the task of providing such ongoing access to old census data sets.

---

[28]The SDSC demonstrations used a relational database to record a subset of metadata information used for finding records.

[29]Note that some subtle aspects of access control arise when indexing or extracting data from collections. A user not authorized to view a record must not see any extracts from that record.

[30]See <http://www.census.gov/main/www/access.html>.

Finding Aids and Search

Over the lifetime of the ERA, access methods can be expected to change. In the last few years, for example, impressive Internet search services have emerged, and users now expect full-text searching to be available for any large collection.

The traditional method of access to archives uses finding aids that describe broad categories of records, for example at the series level. Finding aids are usually based on controlled-vocabulary metadata, for example, MARC AMC and Encoded Archival Description (EAD).[31] Controlled-vocabulary descriptors are assigned manually to information objects, usually at ingest, which makes ingest a more labor-intensive process. NARA has invested considerable resources in describing records series in accordance with uniform practices.[32]

The traditional method of cataloging information and providing access is designed for archives of physical media (e.g., paper, pictures, movies). Different methods of cataloging and access are possible with electronic records, and NARA should include these methods in its planning.

Recent practice in the use of controlled-vocabulary metadata uses automated or semi-automated assignment of descriptors to information objects. One example is text categorization techniques used to assign subject codes to newswire articles,[33] diagnostic codes to patient discharge summaries, and grades to practice GMAT exams.[34] Studies show that current techniques assign descriptors as accurately as humans for some tasks. Because it is not limited by human labor, text categorization can be applied inexpensively, so it could be routinely used in an ERA. It can also be used to provide something that the traditional finding aids do not: by assigning metadata to individual records, which would be prohibitively expensive if done manually, NARA could provide significantly enhanced access at the individual record level.

Finding aids based on full-text search have been developed by the Digital Library and Information Retrieval research communities,[35] and are being adopted commercially, for example by WestLaw.[36] Given a query, the available archives are ranked by how well their

---

[31]See, respectively, the MARC Standards home page, at <http://www.loc.gov/marc/>, and the EAD standard's home page, at <http://www.loc.gov/ead/>.

[32]As of 2002, only 20 percent of "NARA's vast holdings are described in ARC," NARA's online catalog system. See <http://www.archives.gov/research_room/arc>.

[33]Yiming Yang and Xin Liu. 1999. "A Re-examination of Text Categorization Methods." *Proceedings of ACM SIGIR Conference on Research and Development in Information Retrieval* (SIGIR'99), pp. 42-49.

[34]Leah S. Larkey. 1998. "Automated Essay Grading Using Text Categorization Techniques." *Proceedings of the 21st Annual International ACM SIGIR Conference on Research and Development in Information Retrieval* (SIGIR'98), Melbourne, Australia, pp. 90-95.

[35]Luis Gravano and Hector Garcia-Molina. 1995. "Generalizing GlOSS to Vector-Space Databases and Broker Hierarchies." *Proceedings of the 21st International Conference on Very Large Data Bases* (VLDB 1995); L. Gravano, P. Ipeirotis, and M. Sahami. In press. "QProber: A System for Automatic Classification of Hidden-Web Databases." *ACM Transactions on Information Systems*; Jamie Callan. 2000. "Distributed Information Retrieval," in *Advances in Information Retrieval*, W.B. Croft, ed., Kluwer Academic Publishers, Boston, Mass., pp. 127-150.

[36]Jack G. Conrad, Xi S. Guo, Peter Jackson, and Monem Meziou. 2002. "Database Selection Using Actual Physical and Acquired Logical Collection Resources in a Massive Domain-specific Operational Environment." *Proceedings of the 28th International Conference on Very Large Data Bases* (VLDB 2002); Jack G. Conrad and Joanne R.S. Claussen. Forthcoming in 2003. "Early User-System Interaction for Database Selection in Massive Domain-Specific Online Environments." *ACM Transactions on Information Systems*.

contents match the query. This type of finding aid supports detailed information needs and information needs that controlled-vocabulary metadata do not anticipate.

During the last decade the public has become familiar with full-text search in Web, e-mail, corporate, and personal document databases. It is likely that NARA will eventually be expected to provide full-text search capabilities within its archives. It may also be expected to provide for searches across sets of archives (sometimes called "federated search"), such as across both NARA and presidential library collections.[37] For common record data types, full-text search can be provided inexpensively, with little manual intervention, using commercial software.[38]

Full-text search is merely the simplest form of content search, which may include searching images, sounds, animations, videos, hypermedia structures, etc. At present, full-text retrieval is fairly mature while the technology for content-based retrieval of nontextual materials is still immature but developing quickly. Extensions of simple text search are, however, inevitable and will no doubt be demanded by future users if NARA's holdings evolve to include significant multimedia holdings.

The standard method of cataloging archives has been manual assignment of controlled-vocabulary metadata, and NARA may initially face some resistance in adopting alternatives. However a fairly large body of research comparing full-text and controlled-vocabulary methods over a 35-year period indicates (1) each method works "best" for particular types of information needs, (2) the two approaches provide about the same "average case" effectiveness, and (3) a combination of the two approaches is the most effective solution.[39] The latter conclusion is reflected in the National Library of Medicine's PubMed system, which uses both full-text and controlled-vocabulary indexing.[40]

The cataloging and access methodologies used for physical media (e.g., paper, pictures, movies) are labor-intensive and expensive. Newer, content-based cataloging and access methods designed for digital resources are, in contrast, compute-intensive but increasingly inexpensive as computing becomes cheaper. NARA can exploit this property of electronic records to reduce its costs, to improve its ability to ingest information quickly, and to improve the quality of access services it provides. Traditional cataloging and access methodologies will continue to be needed, but NARA will almost certainly never have sufficient resources to apply them to all of the electronic records worth archiving.

Techniques for automatic metadata assignment and/or building indexes for content search

---

[37]Luo Si and Jamie Callan. 2002. "Using Sampled Data and Regression to Merge Search Engine Results." *Proceedings of the Twenty-Fifth Annual International ACM SIGIR Conference on Research and Development in Information Retrieval*. ACM, Tampere, Finland, pp. 19-26.

[38]If full-text indexing is to be provided, engineering calculations should include the storage required for the index, which can be anywhere from 50 to 300 percent the size of the raw data, depending upon the capabilities one wants to offer. Of course, this information would not be stored in the archive, but rather in the working storage associated with an access system. Also, indexes can be regenerated, so the number of index replicas required is driven by such considerations as performance, not reliability.

[39]Cyril W. Cleverdon. 1967. "The Cranfield Tests on Index Language Devices." *Aslib Proceedings* 19: 173-192, reprinted in Karen Sparck Jones and Peter Willett, eds. 1997. *Readings in Information Retrieval*. Morgan Kaufmann, San Francisco; T.B. Rajashekar and W.B. Croft. 1993. "Combining Automatic and Manual Index Representations in Probabilistic Retrieval." *Journal of the American Society for Information Science* 46(4): 272-283.

[40]See <http://www.ncbi.nlm.nih.gov/PubMed/>.

can be applied during ingestion or as a part of the access process. If they can extract essential metadata—i.e., elements that are deemed by NARA to be obligatory for every record—they should be used as part of the ingest process. However, since these techniques are being improved rapidly, it is probably wise to defer their broad use to the time of access, when more modern techniques are available. Metadata extraction or index generation can be applied, if desired, as a collection is staged from the archival file system.

At a minimum, the ERA and NARA overall should provide for full-text searching of all finding aids for its holdings regardless of physical format or data type. The Archival Research Catalog is a step in the right direction, but it is incomplete, especially with regard to electronic records.[41]

Access to Underlying Digital Files

While most users will want access to screen presentations of records or to modest numbers of digital files represented in common data types (e.g., word-processor documents, database tables), some researchers can benefit from access to the elements of the underlying data model used by the ERA. For example, researchers who reverse engineer obscure data types, explore automatic metadata extraction, or devise new methods for content searching (especially on difficult data types such as images, video clips, or executable files) will probably wish for access to the files stored in the archive without mediation or modification (subject, of course, to suitable access controls). These researchers will also make use of data type specifications, metadata definitions, and other information available from the archive that describes the details of the data model used to store records.

SECURITY AND ACCESS CONTROL

Security will need to be carefully designed into the NARA system to address all of the usual concerns about unauthorized access to systems and vulnerability to denial-of-service attacks or to natural or manmade disasters.

These security concerns must be addressed from the very beginning of system design. As an illustration of this principle, consider the basic question of whether the data in the ERA should be stored in cleartext or should be encrypted to prevent inadvertent disclosure of restricted information to the staff and vendors who are in frequent contact with the archive. If stored in cleartext, it is virtually certain that there will be one or more instances of compromised data over the (very long) life of the ERA.[42] However, archivists are reluctant to encrypt data for fear that future generations might lose the key and thus all access to the data. Note that either approach entails risks.

To decide whether it is worth the cost and operational overhead (especially to ensure that

---

[41]As of this writing, only one electronic data file series is included in the ARC.

[42]For example, reports surfaced in late 2002 of the theft of 500,000 medical records by stealing hard disks from a Defense Department contractor. See Associated Press, 2003, "Military, Family Medical Files Stolen," *Washington Times*, January 1. Available online at <http://www.washtimes.com/national/20030101-94263751.htm>.

keys are not lost) of encrypting the data is a difficult question that requires careful analysis. A cryptographically protected archive is a much more difficult design than cleartext, since one needs to worry about key storage and distribution, which pieces of the system operate encrypted and which in the clear, which pieces need to have access to keys, the performance of decryption, and so forth. These decisions will have many ramifications in the details of the design, e.g., the module interfaces.

On the other hand, converting from cleartext to encrypted would require recopying the entire archive. This is a massive undertaking, especially because it will take quite a while and one does not want archive operations (for either ingest or access) to be hampered for such a period. Accordingly, this decision is better made at the outset than being retrofitted later on.

Addressing this and other related security issues is part of a comprehensive system design. There are reasonably well-understood methodologies for doing the threat analysis and working the results into system requirements and design. Indeed, in many respects, the ERA's security issues can be handled by straightforward application of engineering best practices. These issues are not discussed in detail in this initial report, and the reader is referred to the extensive literature on computer system security.[43]

In contrast to many digital libraries, the ERA must control access to many of its records. Access controls are comprised of three basic ingredients:

- *A way to authenticate users who wish access, i.e., to verify their identity.*[44] What are the requirements for authentication?[45] Does every user need to be identified individually, or as a member of a class, e.g., "Internet visitor?"[46]
- *Properties of individual records or collections of records, recorded as metadata with the records, that indicate what kind of access is permitted.*
- *A set of rules that checks whether a certain user may access a certain record.* The rules may cover large classes of records, e.g., "Allow access to a record labeled 'by citizen owner' only if the value of the metadata tag named 'social security number' matches the property 'social security number' of the authenticated user." Or the rules may be very specific, e.g., "John Wright has access to record NARA/ERA/Vietnam-72/104567."

---

[43] An overview of cybersecurity issues is provided in Computer Science and Telecommunications Board, National Research Council, 2002, *Cybersecurity Today and Tomorrow: Pay Now or Pay Later.* National Academy Press, Washington, D.C. An in-depth examination of trustworthiness issues and research challenges is provided in CSTB, NRC, 1999, *Trust in Cyberspace,* National Academy Press, Washington, D.C.

[44] NARA is understandably reluctant to tackle the problem of authenticating all the principals who may have created government records (for example, by recording digital signatures with records and keeping enough information to check signatures many years later). However, there is no reason to avoid authenticating users of an archiving system. Experience elsewhere in the government, such as the Department of Defense's DoD Common Access Card program, may help arrive at an appropriate design.

[45] These and related issues are discussed in National Research Council, 2003, *Who Goes There? Authentication Through the Lens of Privacy,* The National Academies Press, Washington, D.C.

[46] For access to public records, privacy considerations may mean that a detailed audit trail should not be retained, especially since there is no risk of a user damaging or stealing the only copy of an electronic record. So there may be a requirement to authenticate users to classes such as "general public" or "Internet visitor" rather than for individual identification.

In the ERA, these access rules will be complex and may change owing to the passage of time, specific events (e.g., the death of the person to whom the record belongs or refers), or legislation or court orders. The committee saw no evidence that NARA had begun to formalize access controls in a way that could reasonably be automated in the ERA. Perhaps access controls for NARA's existing archives are suitable and can be easily codified for the ERA, but the committee did not see evidence that this had been done and indeed heard a good deal that suggested otherwise, including extensive use of, and indeed reliance upon, human review just prior to the delivery of physical records from the existing archives. (Note that it is not clear whether this will be required in the ERA.)

One of the very real complications is that substantial numbers (though again, the committee has no quantification here) of records ingested into the ERA will be classified at various levels (in the official sense of government classification: SECRET, TOP SECRET, etc.). In briefings, the committee was told that classified and other national-security information would be physically segregated in separate instances of the ERA reserved for that purpose (that is, using "air gaps"), that it is not a requirement of an ERA system that it be able to hold both classified and unclassified information, and thus it would not have to attempt to deal with multilevel secure systems operation.

Nonetheless, the classification of these records triggers a host of highly specific and highly structured design and operational requirements, which the committee has not examined at all. Here the committee raises only two issues:

- *Does NARA intend to actually build multiple complete and independent ERA systems operating at different levels of classification?* If so how many and of what relative sizes, and what constraints will this put on the ERA procurement strategy? The committee has seen no details on the practicality of this approach.
- *How will declassification be handled?* As declassification occurs, material may need to flow from the various classified versions of the ERA to the unclassified one. In addition, provenance and source metadata will need to be propagated from one such system to another. Situations may also occur where the metadata are unclassified (or classified at a lower level than the actual records), and provision will need to be made for these situations. In addition, there is the situation where metadata can be public and the documents described are awaiting declassification review (for which the backlog is often very long).

As explained above, access controls depend in part on a way to authenticate users. NARA should think through how it wishes to authenticate users of the system, whether all users will need to be authenticated, and how attributes are tied to registered users. NARA should not invent a new technology for authenticating users to a computer system—there are several adequate schemes available already—but should determine how the authentication system is administered and how authenticated user identities are tied to access control rules. For example, how does a new user register for access to the system? How does an existing user apply for augmented access?[47]

---

[47]For a discussion of authentication policies, particularly regarding privacy issues, see National Research Council, 2003, *Who Goes There? Authentication Through the Lens of Privacy*, The National Academies Press, Washington, D.C.

INTEGRITY OF RECORDS

Ensuring the survival, integrity, and authenticity of the records (and accompanying metadata) entrusted to it is at the core of NARA's mission. In a digital environment, achieving these goals becomes considerably more complex and nuanced than has been the case in an environment of paper records; designing appropriate measures is an interdependent mixture of techniques from archival practice on the one hand and computer science, cryptology, and computer security on the other. The committee has not comprehensively investigated these questions in preparing this report, but it is clear that they need much more extensive structural consideration than they seem to have received to date.[48]

One set of questions pertains to the transfer of records agencies to NARA and their ingest into an ERA system. Current NARA practice, as explained to the committee, consists of verifying that the file sent by the agency and the file received by NARA have the same length (the same number of bits); this falls well short of available and commonly used tools that provide much more effective ways of verifying integrity. Human intervention to examine records to see if they are complete, match expected formats, and generally "make sense"—an approach adopted in NARA's current process for ingesting databases—is insufficient to detect bogus records and does not scale up to large volumes of records; automated validation and ingest tools are required.

Common best practice is to use checksums to establish that records have not been tampered with, together with some form of authentication of the record source. For example, transfers could be audited using the following procedure. The ingest protocol for a set of records would include a step in which the donating agency provides a list of records to be given to NARA, each one accompanied by its hash checksum,[49] and a later step in which NARA verifies that each of the records it has received does indeed have the same (recomputed) checksum as the one provided in the earlier step.

Once the files have entered the ERA (along with metadata that explain where they originated and what measures were taken to authenticate the source and to validate the file) it will be necessary to design various processes within the ERA to ensure that the bits are not corrupted while in the custody of the ERA. Checksums are the obvious approach here and can also be used to help protect against software errors.

The survival of records once they have entered the ERA depends on several factors. One is the use of redundant, geographically distributed storage to allow records to survive various sorts of physical catastrophes, accidental or deliberate. The committee has seen little discussion of what the design parameters need to be for redundancy and distribution of storage, and

---

[48] One example of a subtle integrity issue that might arise in the future that the committee did not consider is that of executable records. Can the integrity of executables be safely preserved? What if an executable has an expiration date, time bomb, or some other feature that affects interpretation as a function of time?

[49] A hash checksum for a file is the output of a cryptographic hash function (such as the function SHA-1, standardized by NIST) when it is given the file as input; the crucial property of such a function is that it is presumed to be computationally infeasible to find any other input that produces the same output. Therefore this output can serve as a characteristic digital fingerprint for the file, which can easily be recomputed at will and checked against the expected value.

whether these parameters will vary from one class of records to the next. A detailed threat and requirements analysis is needed in this area.

The integrity of records once within the ERA also depends on the design and operation of effective computer security measures as part of the ERA to ensure that unauthorized people cannot add, delete, or alter objects within the ERA. Hash checksums, independently maintained, can offer a second line of defense for at least detection (if not necessarily repair) of alterations, be they due to attacks or accidental failures of the types discussed earlier.

However, in order to protect against malevolent change, the hash value associated with a digital object must be separately protected so that an attacker who manages to gain access to change one cannot also change the other. Since a hash value can be written in a relatively small number of digits, one can protect it from change by publishing it in a very public place, such as a classified advertisement in the *New York Times* (which will, a short time after publication, be captured on microfilm that is distributed to many libraries), or by otherwise depositing the hash value in hundreds of libraries. [50]

---

[50] For an archive that contains millions of digital objects, this idea would lead to purchasing an impractically large number of classified ads. A technique is available for combining the hash values of very large numbers of objects—such as the entire archive—and publishing only a single number that can be computed *only* by knowing all of the contents. See section 2.4 of Stuart Haber and W. Scott Stornetta, 1997, "Secure Names for Bit-strings," *Proceedings of the 4th ACM Conference on Computer and Communications Security*, pp. 2-35, ACM Press, New York, April. The technology is offered commercially by Surety, <http://www.surety.com/solutions.php>.

6

Strengthening Information Technology Expertise

Developing and operating the ERA will require technical expertise that NARA now lacks. While NARA recognizes that its growing focus on digital archives will require a culture change and has initiated an associated "change management" program, the need for expertise to launch the project is both urgent and specific. Based on briefings and other interactions with NARA staff, the committee concludes that while there is recognition of the challenges of the ERA program, few NARA staff members appreciate the complexity of building, managing, and operating a production digital archiving system. Multiple paths can help NARA to obtain the necessary expertise.

EXPERTISE TO DESIGN AND EVOLVE THE ERA

As the preceding chapters have outlined, development of the ERA represents a significant technical and management challenge well beyond that of a typical IT system procurement. NARA has a few staff in leadership roles who appreciate the significant technical challenges of the ERA program. However, briefings to the committee suggest that NARA today does not have sufficient technical depth to assure success in launching the ERA program—that is, to define and manage the overall architecture, develop the appropriate request for proposals (RFP), evaluate technical responses, negotiate changes in the architecture with vendors, and manage the implementation of the system.

Recognizing the need for additional IT expertise in the ERA program office, NARA has supplemented the office with a small cadre of contractor technical staff who are working on ERA design and technical management issues. The documents and briefings received by the committee to date show some in progress identifying desired features of the ERA and some of its associated technical and organizational challenges. But these documents, although useful early steps in system development, are a long way from the detailed engineering analysis and architecture definition that are critically needed.

NARA needs a small staff that holds complete technical knowledge of the ERA. Even if the system is built and augmented by contractors, an in-house contract monitoring staff (e.g., the contracting officer's technical representative) is required that is technically at least as good as the contractor's people. This staff is essential to developing a basic system design and implementation strategy, preparing an RFP, evaluating proposals, monitoring contract progress, and managing system deployment.

Highly skilled staff will be critical to managing the evolution of the ERA. Chapter 7 recommends an iterative development approach for the ERA designed to reduce technical risk by exposing unforeseen problems and overlooked requirements earlier in the software development process and by providing flexibility in reacting to them. However, because this added flexibility requires an active procurement process and an active management style, it also demands particular management skills. For example, because system components can be contracted at a smaller granularity, contracts must be written to provide flexibility, because requirements and designs for each system component are subject to revision. Not only are there more (but smaller) projects to specify and manage, but the management must also have considerable technical sophistication to recognize technical limitations, to determine new requirements, to identify what should be evolved or replaced and when, etc. The increased flexibility of iterative design helps avoid or correct mistakes but requires deep technical understanding of the system as it evolves. Also, short design cycles require frequent testing, frequent deployment of new systems, frequent comparison of alternatives, frequent tuning of system requirements and goals, and frequent interaction with users.

Since ERA systems and their basic architecture will change over time—owing to both iterative development and improved understanding of the requirements as experience is gained—it will be essential for ERA staff to be expert on their technical properties as they evolve. For this reason, NARA should plan to hire permanent staff having this expertise, although short-term contractors or consultants may also help build a critical mass of expertise to launch the ERA program.

The complexity and novelty of the ERA require that the key IT staff have a breadth of expertise in areas such as the following:

- Developing modern IT systems using networked heterogeneous elements;
- Web-based access techniques, including scaling to meet variable and increasing loads;
- Operating large-scale systems, and a knowledge of elements of their design that allow robust, continuous operation;
- Working with digital media and file formats, including content searching; and
- Security.

Staff with this expertise might be recruited from developers of digital libraries or other online information-retrieval services. To address the kinds of issues laid out in this report, this staff would ideally have an understanding of digital archival issues.

The committee recognizes the challenges facing NARA or any other federal agency in recruiting and retaining IT talent.[1] However, the need for key staff is urgent if NARA is to

---

[1]For a discussion of human resource issues related to IT expertise in the context of the Library of Congress, see Computer Science and Telecommunications Board, National Research Council, 2001, *LC21: A Digital Strategy for the Library of Congress*, National Academy Press, Washington, D.C. Available online at <http://books.nap.edu/catalog/9940.html>.

stick to its current implementation plan, because their expertise is needed in order to formulate an architecture and RFP(s), evaluate responses, select one or more contractors, and begin development.

External Advice

NARA should seek ongoing advice from the outside to ensure the success of its ERA development. NARA currently has several advisory committees, but none with a concentration of expertise in electronic records archiving. Indeed, the Advisory Committee on Preservation has only one member who is directly involved in digital preservation. The underlying technologies associated with electronic records and their preservation continue to change rapidly, making it important to seek out high-level strategic advice continually. The appropriate expertise can be found in several areas, including the digital library community, government and commercial operators of online information-retrieval services, and the research community.

Advisors can help chart the course of the ERA. For example, as noted above, external review of the overall ERA architecture would be valuable. Ideally, advisors could also help craft RFPs and evaluate the proposals responding to them. A strong advisory board might also help recruit the necessary senior staff and might spin off more in-depth study groups focusing on particular technical issues.

EXPERTISE TO OPERATE THE ERA

Operating the electronic records archiving systems, as distinct from specifying and developing them, will require strengthening the IT skills of NARA's staff. Some of these skills will focus on the following:

- Managing the hardware and software resources of electronic records archiving systems, including setting up procedures for testing new software releases, for auditing the data stored in the archive, for incorporating new hardware (e.g., disks), for scheduling media refresh and consequent decommissioning of old disks, and so forth. The critical preservation responsibilities of NARA place the highest technical demands on staff who manage the system.
- Operating an online service to access electronic collections, including such activities as accommodating varying loads (i.e., scaling up services to respond to public demand) and defending against possible malicious attacks arriving via the public network.
- Wide-ranging problem-solving associated with ingesting records. Skilled people will be needed to solve problems posed by old and incomplete digital data transferred from agencies: extracting useful data, checking its integrity, figuring out in what forms it should be archived, and so forth. Automating robust procedures for processing large numbers of records or record series that are received on a recurring basis will also require skilled IT people to develop the necessary tools and procedures.

As ERA systems are built and deployed, and as digital records become a major part of NARA's work, much of the staff will need to become savvy and comfortable with digital records and preservation. As the volume of electronic records increases relative to that of conventional paper records, NARA will need an increasing fraction of its archivist staff to have a combination of technical and archival skills and it will need a larger, highly skilled systems administration and technical support staff. Achieving this shift will require a culture change, as NARA has recognized and reflected in its appointment of a change manager.

A critical aspect of NARA's new culture will be that IT must be recognized as a "core competence" that must thrive to support digital preservation. NARA management will have to overcome the tendency to look at electronic records as a special problem that can be shunted to an isolated office where only specialists will handle them. NARA will need far more staff who feel equally confident dealing with paper and electronic records and many more specialists with competence in managing and preserving electronic records. The preponderance of training and technical assistance that NARA provides to agencies should also shift its emphasis from paper records to electronic records. Achieving this sort of agency-wide transformation will be difficult.

7

Strategy for Evolution and Acquisition

Because the ERA must have a long life—many decades—it must evolve over time. Although it is possible to express some of today's requirements for the ERA, others will become clear only as operational experience is gained, and the requirements will themselves evolve. The types of records to be preserved, the interests and capabilities of users, and other aspects of the context will change. So too will the technology available to NARA; computer capabilities and cost-performance evolve very fast, so what is difficult or expensive today can be much easier in 10 years. The sections that follow describe how, even though all the requirements cannot be anticipated, the system can be built using techniques that make evolution easy rather than hard.

STRATEGY FOR EVOLUTION

Modular Design

One of the most important techniques for developing a large system is to modularize—making a complex problem more tractable by breaking it down into a set of smaller components and enabling independent evolution of the pieces over time. NARA and the SDSC have embraced modular design in general and the OAIS overall framework for an archive.[1] The SDSC demonstrations successfully exploit the clear separation of the major modules of ingest, storage, and access.

A modular approach presumes that each modular component will be changed several

---

[1] Consultative Committee for Space Data Systems (CCSDS). 2002. *Reference Model for an Open Archival Information System (OAIS).* CCSDS 650.0-B-1 (Blue Book). CCSDS Secretariat, National Aeronautics and Space Administration, Washington, D.C. January. Available online at <http://wwwclassic.ccsds.org/documents/pdf/CCSDS-650.0-B-1.pdf>.

times as requirements change or more attractive technologies emerge. Properly designed components can be replaced with improved versions with minimal disruption to other modules.

Modularization thus enables considerable flexibility in evolving a system. For example:

- Several prototypes can be built to explore alternative methods of accomplishing a particularly crucial goal.
- Prototypes of individual modules can be discarded without jeopardizing investments made in the rest of the system.
- A sequence of smaller, focused development projects can be used to add capability to the system.
- The design and implementation of different system components can be divided among multiple vendors or research centers with specialized abilities. For example, a modular design should permit developing a new access technique for a particular kind of record without altering other parts of the system.
- Commercial off-the-shelf (COTS) or other third-party packages—for, say, full-text indexing and search—can often be integrated individually into the system.

The hallmarks of modular design are the decomposition of the system into separate modules and the specification of the interfaces that surround each module, i.e., the details of the connections a module makes to other modules in the system. While it would be fairly easy to draw a high-level block diagram showing a modular system structure (such as was done in the OAIS framework[2]), more detailed evaluation of the required modules and interfaces is critical to obtaining the rewards of modular design. If modules are too big, they become hard to change or replace. If the interfaces become too complex or allow internal details of a module's implementation to become known to other modules, the set of modules becomes "brittle," and the ability to change one module independently of others may be lost. The details of modular structure and interface designs are critical.

Possible Modules and Interfaces for the ERA

This section briefly discusses some considerations for modular design of an archive system and outlines some of the possible modules and interfaces that would need to be specified for the ERA. In describing these, the committee intends only to provide some concrete illustrations of issues to be faced in the system design, not to do detailed design work.

To exploit modular structure for incremental evolution, it is necessary to define the software interfaces by which each module connects to other modules. These interfaces require defining subroutine calls and data types transferred between the modules. The data model used to store records in the file system serves in effect as an interface between ingest and access modules: Even though an ingest module does not directly invoke an access module, the

---

[2]ISO Consultative Committee for Space Data Systems (CCSDS). 2002. *Reference Model for an Open Archival Information System (OAIS)*. CCSDS 650.0-B-1 (Blue Book). CCSDS Secretariat, National Aeronautics and Space Administration, Washington, D.C. January. Available online at <http://wwwclassic.ccsds.org/documents/pdf/CCSDS-650.0-B-1.pdf>.

data created by any ingest module must be precisely understood by every corresponding access module.

Modular structure is also used for another purpose: to develop sets of modules that perform related functions. For example, the ERA might have a set of access modules and choose one to invoke based on the collection the user has requested. Similarly, a data-type converter is selected and invoked based on the types of its input and output.

The following are among the likely key interfaces in the ERA system:

- *The file system interface.* This interface provides functions to manipulate files in the repository: naming, reading, writing, access control, etc.[3]
- *The ingest module interface.* The principal role of an ingest module is to prepare and write data into the file system. However, a detailed system design will uncover other interfaces—for example, for tracking records as part of work flow management.
- *The access module interface.* Access modules will be used to build indexes of collections and to query previously built indexes. Access modules will need access to any files that are copied from the main file system into a cache.
- *The data model and associated interface.* These are for manipulating stored data according to the data model.

One objective of defining these interfaces is to allow multiple ingest and access modules to be written without disrupting other parts of the system.

There are also important smaller modules and their corresponding interfaces. For example, the following are likely to be required:

- *Data-type converters*, which transform data from one type into another. Converters may be used within ingest modules to generate derived forms, or within access modules to generate the data type requested by the user or necessary for preparing a visual presentation.
- *Data-type checkers*, which are simply a variant of data-type converters. They are used by ingest modules to verify the integrity of native and derived forms.
- *Metadata extractors*, which derive metadata from records. They may be used within ingest modules to derive metadata for records being ingested, or they may be used by indexers to extract metadata that are useful for searching a set of records.
- *Indexers* used by access modules to (1) prepare an index to a set of records and (2) respond to search queries.

There are certainly many others.

---

[3]Strictly speaking, the use of the term "file" assumes a particular architecture—specifically that the archive lives on a file system and not on, say, a database. It also assumes that the file system does not have, for example, multiple resource forks per file (i.e., on some systems, you can have one logical file, but within it, you might have separate ways of accessing it that give you the data, the metadata, an alternative view, etc). The term file is used in this report to stand for some sort of stored object or item, which may not necessarily actually be a file stored on a conventional file system.

Architecture

An architecture specification is an essential part of the long-term plan for evolving a system. It is the architecture of the system that ensures that the pieces fit together, that the system can be incrementally upgraded, and that it can evolve over time. The architecture needs to specify the interfaces between major parts using an open approach that allows multiple vendors to supply components over a long lifetime. It needs to be nonmonolithic, employing the modular structure discussed above. An example of a digital preservation architecture sketch in this spirit is that of the Library of Congress' National Digital Information Infrastructure Preservation Program (NDIIPP).[4]

A common architecture is especially important for a complex program such as the ERA, which must unify multiple systems. By building early iterations of these systems to be compliant with a common architectural framework, these systems can coalesce into a smaller number of more comprehensive systems as experience and confidence grow.

Because changing the modular structure is far harder than evolving separate modules, devising a good initial architecture for the earliest deployed systems is important. But no matter how good the initial design, it will be subject to evolution over time as requirements are better understood or new requirements emerge.

The architecture of a system like the ERA should be "owned"—that is, specified and evolved over time—by its user. By building the internal expertise to perform this process itself, NARA will better understand the implications of alternative proposals, maintain better control over the development process, and be better able to use the resulting system and understand its limitations and strengths as it is delivered. By owning the architecture, NARA also reduces its dependence on the vendors selected to build implementations of the ERA and helps to avoid proprietary lock-in.

Preparing the architectural design of the ERA requires first-class talent having both archival and IT expertise. So too does managing the inevitable evolution over time to meet new requirements. Thus in both the short and long terms, NARA staff will need to understand deeply the IT aspects of the ERA systems and of digital preservation more generally.

Alternatively, NARA could contract for one or more architectural designs. This is a poor alternative to a NARA-owned architecture. It also does not relieve NARA of the need for first-class technical talent, for NARA would still have to specify the scope of a design contract, evaluate resulting designs, and proceed with acquiring and evolving a system. In this alternative, it might be worthwhile to obtain several proposals, because different contractors may have different technology opportunities, different ideas for incorporating COTS elements, and so forth.

NARA will need to carefully evaluate the one or more architectures it commissions. It may wish to seek the help of outside experts or others with similar needs (e.g., Library of Congress, National Library of Medicine, and other operators of digital libraries) to help in the evaluation. NARA might also choose to contract for help in evaluating multiple architectural proposals.

---

[4]National Digital Information Infrastructure and Preservation Program, Library of Congress. 2003. *NDIIPP Plan Appendix.* Library of Congress, Washington, D.C. Available online at <http://www.digitalpreservation.gov/ndiipp/repor/ndiipp_appendix.pdf>.

Some Other Strategies for Long System Life

Special considerations need to be given to ensuring that the ERA can continue to operate over many decades. Even if the system's requirements were to remain invariant over such a long time, the COTS hardware and software on which the system runs would need to be replaced many times. The design of the system can simplify this process. In addition to modularity, discussed above, the following design ideas will facilitate long-term operation:

- *Use networks based on Internet Protocol (IP) to interconnect hardware components.* The structure of hardware components should allow flexible interconnection of hardware from various vendors using standard networking hardware and protocols—e.g., IP.[5] Replacing old hardware with new, or adding hardware capacity is a matter of attaching the new hardware to the network and perhaps changing the network configuration. Although the physical layers of networks will evolve over time to increase performance—from Ethernet to gigabit Ethernet to 10-gigabit Ethernet and beyond—routers will connect the different physical layers into a single network. The Internet protocols may change, but very slowly, and with evolutionary support from hardware and system software vendors. IP-based networks are the best bet for long-term hardware interconnection.

- *Design software to simplify porting to new hardware and software systems.* Over the life of the ERA, software that implements the ERA will need to be deployed on new computers, perhaps computers that are not completely compatible, either in hardware or software, with the older computers. Writing portable software is a fairly common practice; it involves choosing appropriate programming languages and isolating hardware and software system dependencies in small "compatibility layers" of software.

- *Avoid proprietary lock-in and choose truly common COTS products.* NARA will need to retain sufficient intellectual property rights for the software it procures for the ERA system to be sure that the ERA software can be modified and ported to new hardware and software platforms. Likewise, interfaces and data types that play essential roles in the modular structure (and therefore, evolution) of the system should be free of proprietary features that might trap NARA into hiring only a particular contractor that holds the necessary intellectual property rights.

In designing the architecture of the ERA, NARA wisely wishes to make use of COTS hardware and software products. Because of the long-lifetime objective of the ERA architecture, however, COTS components will have to be chosen with care to be sure that they, or equivalent replacements, are available for a long time. COTS hardware, including storage media, is essential. Trade-offs may be required between (1) using a few large off-the-shelf software components, which will facilitate system integration but may introduce critical dependencies affecting the system's future viability should the components cease to be sold or supported, and (2) using a larger number of smaller components that could be replaced with custom versions if necessary. One way to achieve some flexibility is to partially insulate the

---

[5]Note that the fact that the components of the system use Internet protocols to interconnect internally is separate from the question of whether the NARA ERA is connected directly to the Internet.

ERA architecture from the details of a particular COTS offering by specifying a simple, generic interface, which is then attached to a specific COTS product with a shim (driver)—this idea is commonly used in operating systems and is used in the Storage Request Broker in the SDSC work.

COTS modules must be chosen carefully to be valuable to a long-lived system. COTS offerings with a large market—truly *common* products—and slowly changing specifications (perhaps today's operating systems and network-attached file systems are examples) can probably be replaced with compatible or similar products for many years. But low-volume COTS modules involve risk: If, say, NARA were to buy a single vendor's document management system to implement a major portion of the ERA, there might be no other COTS source for upgrades or replacements. Generally, COTS components are easier to build into systems with short lifetimes than long-lived systems such as the ERA.[6]

These strategies all depend on judgments about the expected life of hardware and software components. In extreme cases, modules may need to be redesigned or rewritten to replace components no longer available. But without modular structure and nonproprietary interfaces it will be far harder to keep the system running smoothly over a long period.

ITERATIVE (SPIRAL) DEVELOPMENT

A series of implementations is built, fashioned to acquire experience with an initial system and then incorporate improvements—this technique is called "iterative design." When precise requirements are not known in advance, the detailed requirements may be elicited by undertaking a series of iterative designs in which development follows a cycle of specify, design, implement, and operate. An explicit iterative design goal is to keep the cycles short—to complete a single cycle in months, not years. At each iteration of the cycle, the architecture is refined.

Military procurements call this technique "spiral development," in reference to how requirements are refined and expanded as a result of experience with earlier, simpler systems.[7] Iterative design allows users to operate a partially working system, or partially working system components, early in the development process. The approach provides rapid feedback about what works, what doesn't, what needs to be refined or rejected, and what is missing.

The initial systems usually have modest expectations; they gather experience to inform the next iteration. The initial systems are put in operation and subjected to a range of uses and tests in order to obtain as much experience as possible to influence subsequent iterations. This form of deliberate, rapid evolution is used to refine the initial set of requirements. Eventually, the requirements will become well understood.

In contrast to a more conventional procurement, the ERA program will also have to man-

---

[6]There are, of course, many other issues associated with the use of COTS and other trade-offs between using custom and off-the-shelf software. These are not discussed in this report.

[7]See, for example, Barry Boehm (edited by Wilfred J. Hansen), 2000, "Spiral Development: Experience, Principles, and Refinements," Special Report CMU/SEI-2000SR-008, *Spiral Development Workshop* (February 9, 2000), Carnegie Mellon Software Engineering Institute, Pittsburgh, Pa. Available online at <http://www.sei.cmu.edu/cbs/spiral2000/february2000/BoehmSR.html>.

age the evolution of the requirements themselves by virtue of the very long life of the ERA program. Requirements will inevitably change as electronic records evolve, new techniques for using records emerge, new preservation techniques become available, and so forth. Planning for the ERA program should, therefore, anticipate a sustained iterative development process.

Experience shows that an iterative design will be required to arrive at the best modular design for the ERA. While the very-high-level structure—with separate ingest, storage, and access components—is likely to change little, the detailed interface designs will evolve. With the present level of experience in the archiving community, it is possible to craft a good initial design but to not be assured it is correct. The modularity and interfaces themselves will have to be improved by iteration as requirements are better understood and change.

PILOTS: STARTING SMALL AND GAINING EXPERIENCE

An important early stage of the iterative development process is the building of "pilots"—systems that are sufficiently small and simple that they can be rapidly deployed but capable enough for production use. A pilot is relatively small compared with the ultimate system, meaning that its cost is also relatively small and that any failures that occur in the earliest stages have only modest consequences for the program as a whole. The crucial difference between pilots and "prototypes" is that pilots, unlike prototypes, are designed with enough functionality and sufficient scale to be operated in a production environment, allowing real-world experience to be gained that informs the requirements of later, more capable iterations of the system. This sort of staged approach is being used for the electronic deposit system at the Netherlands national library (Box 7.1).

For a program as complex as the ERA, it is very useful to "sample" the problem space by launching several pilots concurrently. Each pilot provides experience with different aspects of the full problem; each pilot also offers opportunities to try different approaches to particular elements of the problem.

Although the pilots will differ from one another in some respects, all the pilot systems should be constructed within a common architectural framework. By working within a common framework, the pilot systems can, in subsequent design iterations, eventually coalesce into a smaller number of more comprehensive systems as experience and confidence grow.

It is especially important that the data model—the data types and related metadata—used in each pilot conform to a common architecture so that the digital data obtained by ingesting records into one of the early systems will carry forward into future evolutions.[8] At some system iteration it may be necessary to rebuild the archive according to a new data model (especially if the data model is changed significantly), reading all the records archived using the old model, converting to the new model, and writing a new archive. This scenario—the wholesale reformatting of the archive—should be possible with early designs.

---

[8]No matter how well the data model is defined at the outset, it is still likely to change as the system design is iteratively refined. To minimize the disruptions caused by such changes, version numbers should be made explicit in the data model. In this way, the ERA software can respond to a range of versions correctly, rather than requiring the entire archive to be converted to a new data model when versions change.

> **BOX 7.1**
> **Staged Implementation of the Electronic Deposit System at the Netherlands National Library**
>
> A recent example of a staged implementation is the Electronic Deposit system at the Netherlands national library—the Koninklijke Bibliotheek (KB) in the Hague—the first operational system of this kind in the world. Its goal is to archive for the long term all documents electronically published in the Netherlands. In 2000, the KB issued an RFP and then signed a development contract with IBM in the fall. A previous study had already recommended that the program (1) use the OAIS reference model and (2) focus entirely on document storage and retrieval functions, while leaving to the library system (already in existence) the responsibility for cataloguing, indexing, and search. The system was built following these recommendations. Using a tape robot, optical library, and RAID disk system, it relies as much as possible on off-the-shelf products (e.g., IBM Content Manager; Tivoli Storage Manager, a backup and archive system; and DB2, a database management system). The design objectives call for 20 TB in 2005, with a long-term objective of 500 TB. The system was delivered in fall 2002. In parallel, several joint KB-IBM studies were conducted,[1] most of them on actual preservation issues. Their results will fuel the next development stage, in which some preservation functionality will be added to the system.
>
> ---
> [1] IBM-Koninklijke Bibliotheek (KB). 2002. *IBM-Koninklijke Bibliotheek Long-Term Preservation Study.* Koninklijke Bibliotheek, The Hague.

Experience with the pilot systems can be expected to lead to changes to the architecture and to substantial refinement of requirements for subsequent, more comprehensive systems. Successfully building on the pilot experience will require skill in developing an initial architecture, managing the first system developments, learning from early operations, making revisions to architecture and specifications, and evolving the overall program.

ERA pilots should exploit available collections of records that could be organized and made available quickly, and they should sample different dimensions of the overall archiving challenge. NARA will need to choose a limited set of objectives for the pilot systems. Examples of some of the limitations on archive content might be these:

- Deal only with records already held by NARA by reingesting them into a new system.
- Select a single collection.
- Select a single agency with a limited set of scheduled digital records.
- Select a diverse collection but provide the best access only to the six most common data types.
- Select a small collection that has challenging ingest problems because of old media, old software, unknown data types, etc.

Here are some specific examples of limited-scope systems that might be considered for early ERA pilots:

- *U.S. State Department cables.* NARA is preparing to acquire digital forms of State Department diplomatic cables, which are simple text files. One pilot might focus on preserving these cables, extracting appropriate metadata automatically from the cables, perhaps providing full-text search, or other access appropriate to the collection. For quickest deployment, NARA might consider making these records available using software already developed for operating a digital library.
- *Records at the National Personnel Records Center.* Military personnel records, traditionally stored on paper or microfilm, have more recently been managed by the Department of Defense as TIFF image files. There is interest in preserving these records in electronic form when they are transferred to NARA's National Personnel Records Center. Containing millions of service and medical records of discharged and deceased veterans, these collections are large but homogeneous. Use and access considerations would be quite different than for the State Department cables because of confidentiality protections and the imperative to provide ready access to veterans or next of kin. Access controls would be required.
- *E-mail from the Clinton administration held by the Clinton Presidential Center.* This collection would lead to experience with a broader and more modern range of data types, because it contains e-mail attachments of all sorts. Metadata could be extracted from the e-mail headers, full-text search could be provided, and so forth. This pilot would provide useful information on the range of data types attached to e-mail and how best to preserve and access these records.

Appendixes

A

Background on NARA and the ERA Program

This appendix, which is drawn entirely from various National Archives and Records Administration publications, has been prepared to provide the reader with some background on NARA, its conceptualization and plans for the ERA program, and related matters. The committee feels that it would be more effective, particularly given the time constraints under which the report was prepared, to let NARA speak for itself on these issues.

BACKGROUND ON NARA'S MISSION FROM THE NARA WEB SITE AND THE NARA STRATEGIC PLAN

What Is NARA?

The National Archives and Records Administration (NARA) is an independent federal agency that preserves our nation's history and defines us as a people by overseeing the management of all federal records.[1]

NARA's Mission

NARA ensures, for the citizen and the public servant, for the President and for the Congress and the Courts, ready access to essential evidence.[2]

---

[1] National Archives and Records Administration (NARA). Undated. "What Is The National Archives & Records Administration?" Available online at <http://www.archives.gov/about_us/what_is_nara/what_is_nara.html>.

[2] National Archives and Records Administration (NARA). Undated. "NARA's Vision, Mission, and Values." Available online at <http://www.archives.gov/about_us/vision_mission_values.html>.

What Does NARA Do?

The National Archives and Records Administration is our national record keeper. It is a public trust that safeguards the records on which people of a democratic republic depend for documenting their individual rights, for ensuring the accountability and credibility of their national institutions, and for analyzing their national experience. Both the Government and the public rely on NARA to meet an almost unlimited range of information needs from records. Such records are essential for congressional oversight committees to evaluate agencies, for veterans to prove their entitlements to such benefits as medical care, for citizens to discover their families' histories, and for Holocaust survivors to trace assets looted from them by the Nazis. These are just a few of the many uses made of U.S. Government records. The records we preserve and make available every day directly affect the lives of millions of our citizens as well as the understanding we have of our nation's history.[3]

NARA's Responsibilities

NARA is responsible for issuing records management guidance; working with agencies to implement effective controls over the creation, maintenance, and use of records in the conduct of agency business; providing oversight of agencies' records management programs; and providing storage facilities for certain temporary agency records. The Federal Records Act also authorizes NARA to conduct inspections of agency records and records management programs.

NARA works with agencies to identify and inventory records, appraise their value, and determine whether they are temporary or permanent, how long the temporary records should be kept, and under what conditions both the temporary and permanent records should be kept. This process is called scheduling. No record may be destroyed unless it has been scheduled, and for temporary records the schedule is of critical importance because it provides the authority to dispose of the record after a specified time period. Records are governed by schedules that are specific to an agency or by a general records schedule, which covers records common to several or all agencies. According to NARA, records covered by general records schedules make up about a third of all federal records. For the other two thirds, NARA and the agencies must agree upon specific records schedules. Once a schedule has been approved, the agency must issue it as a management directive, train employees in its use, apply its provisions to temporary and permanent records, and evaluate the results.[4]

Scheduling Records

NARA designates records as permanent if they have sufficient historical or other value to warrant their continued preservation by the Government. Such records may be kept mainly because they document an agency's origins, organization, functions, and significant transac-

---

[3]National Archives and Records Administration (NARA). 2000 (revised). *Ready Access to Essential Evidence: The Strategic Plan of the National Archives and Records Administration 1997-2007*. Available online at <http://www.archives.gov/about_us/strategic_planning_and_reporting/2000_strategic_plan.html>

[4]Government Accounting Office (GAO). 2002. *Information Management: Challenges in Managing and Preserving Electronic Records* (GAO-02-586). GAO, Washington, D.C., June. Available online at <http://www.gao.gov/cgi-bin/getrpt?GAO-02-586>.

tions and activities. Or they may be kept mainly because they document the persons, places, things, or matters dealt with by an agency; that is, because they contain information with significant research or reference value.

[...]

Comparatively few records are permanent, although the exact proportion varies from agency to agency and from office to office.[5]

BACKGROUND ON THE ELECTRONIC RECORDS ARCHIVES PROGRAM

From the Mission Needs Statement

The National Archives and Records Administration (NARA) ensures, for the private citizen and all branches of the Government, ready access to essential evidence that documents the rights of citizens, the actions of Federal officials, and the national experience. NARA is a public trust which plays a key role in fostering effective and responsible government through management of the lifecycle of records in all three branches of the Federal Government and through sustained access to historically valuable records in the National Archives and the Presidential Libraries. These records enable people to inspect what the Government has done, allow officials and agencies to review their actions, and help citizens hold the Government accountable. These records are rich and varied sources of information that Americans use to answer questions they have about our past.

Increasingly, these records are created and maintained in electronic formats. To continue to fulfill its mission, NARA needs to respond effectively to the challenge posed by the diversity, complexity, and enormous volume of electronic records being created today and the rapidly changing nature of the systems that are used to create them. Electronic records pose unique difficulties including ease of erasure and advancing technology that renders records and operating systems obsolete in a short period of time. The greatest challenge to managing and preserving electronic records is that the environment is dynamic and unpredictable. America is only at the beginning of "e-government." Technology will continue to change. Citizens, businesses and government agencies at all levels will increasingly use computers and networks. Undoubtedly, they will profit from improvements in technology to develop new and better ways to do business, and these will produce new types of electronic records and recordkeeping systems. But no one knows exactly how these things will evolve.

Regardless of what the future brings, proper records will be needed to support the efficient functioning of the Government, to protect the rights of individuals and businesses, and to ensure that the Government is accountable to its citizens. Thus the challenge of electronic records is that of open-ended change played out against an enduring need. The solution itself must be dynamic, capable of responding to continuing change, and it must be sound, ensuring that electronic records delivered to future generations of Americans are as accurate decades in

---

[5]National Archives and Records Administration (NARA). 2000. *Disposition of Federal Records: A Records Management Handbook* (2000 Web Edition of 1997 printed publication), NARA, Washington, D.C., Chapter 4. Available online at <http://www.archives.gov/records_management/publications/disposition_of_federal_records/chapter_4.html>.

the future as they were when first created. Unless we can solve the technological challenge of preserving electronic records, NARA will be unable to meet its statutory mission.[6]

[...]

Increasingly, our society does business by computer. To the extent that we rely on information technology in the course of our affairs, we must be able to rely on the electronic records that are the instruments and by-products of our activities. We must be able to access and use them effectively in the continuing conduct of affairs. We must be able to rely on them to define and assert our rights, and to hold our public officials accountable. Long after the needs of current affairs have been met, the essential records must serve the interests of future generations in understanding our national experience.

ERA will be a comprehensive, systematic, and dynamic means for preserving virtually any kind of electronic record, free from dependence on any specific hardware or software. When operational, ERA will make it easy for NARA customers to find records they want and easy for NARA to deliver those records in formats suited to customers' needs. Moreover, ERA's technology promises to be useful to many kinds of archives, libraries, agencies, and businesses, regardless of size. ERA will preserve essential evidence and make it more accessible in every sector of society.[7]

From NARA's "ERA Vision Statement"

ERA will authentically preserve and provide access to any kind of electronic record, free from dependency on any specific hardware or software, enabling NARA to carry out its mission into the future.

Vivid Description

1. We will be a leader in innovation in electronic records archiving.

2. In coordination with our Federal partners, we will develop policy and technical guidance to enable responsible electronic records creation and management.

3. With help from our research partners, we will develop and maintain the technical capability to capture, preserve, describe, access and appropriately dispose of any government electronic record.

4. We will manage a coherent, nationwide, and sustainable system for permanent archival electronic records of the Federal Government.

5. We will develop the capability to manage Federal agency electronic records within the NARA records center system.

---

[6]National Archives and Records Adminstration (NARA), 2002, "Electronic Records Archives: Mission Needs Statement (MNS)," p. 1. Available online at <http://www.archives.gov/electronic_records_archives/about_era/mission.html>.

[7]Ibid., p. 5.

6. We will ensure that anyone, at anytime, from any place, has access to the best tools to find and use the records we preserve.

7. Our staff will be capable and consistent users of the electronic tools at every point of the life cycle.

8. We will sustain widespread support from all our stakeholders and customers by listening to their needs, meeting their requirements, and seeking their feedback.[8]

From NARA's Electronic Records Archives Concept of Operations (ConOps)[9]

Section 1.2, ERA Program Overview

The Archivist of the United States established the ERA Program in NARA Notice 2000-074 to address critical issues in the creation, management, and use of electronic records. As a program, ERA comprises the policies, procedures, practices, and the necessary technology that will enable NARA to build the ERA System to receive, preserve, and provide access to electronic records. The resulting ERA System will be a comprehensive, systematic, and dynamic means for preserving virtually any kind of electronic record, free from dependence on any specific hardware or software. In addition to handling the actual records, ERA also will automate electronic records life cycle management activities. ERA, when operational, will make it easy for NARA customers to find records they want, and easy for NARA to deliver those records in formats suited to customers' needs.

Section 3.0, Current Capability

At this time, NARA's archival processes for electronic records are neither fully automated nor fully integrated. The electronic records collected by NARA over the past quarter century consist primarily of data files and databases. Current accessions of records are increasing in scope, diversity, and volume.

The content and internal structure of the electronic records that are being accessioned reflect a broad spectrum of programs and activities of the Federal Government. Changing technologies support new and different types of data with enhanced formats (e.g., e-mail, geospatial data, digital imagery, office automation products, etc.). In addition, the rapid growth of the Internet is fueling increased public demand for improved on-line access to the electronic records held by NARA. Consequently, all of these factors motivate the need for a system that will adequately preserve electronic records as long as they are needed, while providing access to them.

---

[8]NARA. 2002. "Electronic Records Archives (ERA) Vision Statement." April 18. Available online at <http://www.archives.gov/electronic_records_archives/about_era/vision.html>.

[9]NARA. 2002. "Electronic Records Archives Concept of Operations (ConOps)." October 29. Available online at <http://www.archives.gov/electronic_records_archives/about_era/concept_of_operations.html>.

Section 3.1, Background

NARA is not new to the preservation of electronic records. Three decades ago, the agency developed an electronic records management strategy. Since that time, NARA has used that strategy to accession, preserve, and provide access to a significant number of highly structured electronic records. This strategy calls for the storage of data in a software and hardware-independent format (typically fixed length or delimited files in a standard character set, such as the American Standard Code for Information Interchange (ASCII)), on a master and back-up copy of proven, commercially available storage media.

For the storage of the data that have been accessioned, NARA adheres to prescribed environmental standards, performs annual statistical sampling to guard against any loss of data, and copies the records onto new media before any deterioration of the current media occurs. Historically, media refreshment has occurred on a 10-year cycle.

NARA's current services for providing access to electronic records in its holdings allow researchers to search NARA-created finding aids (in hard copy or on the World Wide Web) to identify what collections are available. NARA then allows researchers to obtain copies of documentation on the structure and content of those collections or to visit NARA's facility in College Park, MD, to review that documentation and purchase copies of entire data sets for their own use. NARA also has made the content of a few of its most frequently requested collections available via the Internet.

Section 3.2, Operational Overview

In NARA's current environment, systems such as the Archival Preservation System (APS) and Archival Electronic Records Inspection And Control (AERIC) system allow it to preserve the bits that make up electronic records and verify the structure and content of a limited number of types of electronic records. When fully implemented the Archives Document Review and Redaction System (ADRRES) and the Unclassified Redaction and Tracking System (URTS) may be instrumental in the access review process for electronic records. In addition, development is underway to support user access through the Archival Research Catalog (ARC) and Access to Archival Databases (AAD) systems. The functional capabilities of the APS, AERIC, ADRRES, URTS, ARC, and AAD systems will be included in the long-term technical solution and suite of information technology (IT) tools for lifecycle management of records. APS, AERIC, and AAD address requirements that are specific to electronic records. These requirements will be addressed within the ERA system itself. Other existing systems address requirements that apply to other types of records. NARA intends to provide interoperability across lifecycle management applications through its target enterprise architecture. For additional information about existing systems, refer to NARA's Baseline Characterization Document (BCD).

[...]

Section 5.0, Concepts for the Proposed System

ERA will take advantage of sound and proven technologies in order to accommodate the volume, diversity, and complexity of electronic records that NARA must address both now and in the future. Managing electronic records requires an integrated, automated process from receipt through final disposition and public access. The increased volume and complexity of the records demands this kind of management. Consequently, the ConOps described in this document stresses urgency for a high-level of automation that will result in changes to the current approach to managing electronic records.

[...]

ERA must be capable of addressing electronic records for which there has been little or no front-end involvement or preparation prior to their transfer by the originating entity. Further, the user scenarios presented in this document recognize that NARA staff may act in the role of the originating entity. While the scenarios assume some degree of front-end involvement, they include the possibility that all transfers may not conform to ERA requirements. Acknowledging that the level of processing and service for nonconforming electronic records may vary, ERA will nevertheless provide a means of preserving and accessing these materials.

[...]

Section 8.0, Analysis of the Proposed ERA

Various benefits, limitations, advantages, and disadvantages of ERA are covered in this section.

Section 8.1, Disadvantages and Limitations

Potential disadvantages or limitations to ERA include:

- High development costs
- High costs associated with security
- NARA staff anxiety brought about by new responsibilities resulting from changes due to electronic records
- Poor NARA staff morale without proactive change management
- Impact on originating entities (resources required to prepare for transfer of materials to NARA, greater records management responsibilities)
- User misunderstanding of ERA's relation to the universe of NARA's holdings

Section 8.2, Summary of Benefits and Advantages

ERA will offer numerous benefits to NARA and record users including:

- The preservation of electronic records that would otherwise be lost
- A wider variety of electronic records in NARA holdings
- Consolidated electronic records administration and streamlined internal workflow
- More front end involvement with originating entities
- Higher quality accessioned electronic records
- New tools to support processing and review of electronic records
    —Tools to aid in review decisions
    —Tools for withdrawal and redaction
    —Tools for description.
- Faster access to electronic records
- The ability to service additional record users
- Increased responsiveness and consistency with record users
- Remote access to electronic records
- Enhanced capabilities for searching electronic records

B

Conclusions from the General Accounting Office Report *Information Management: Challenges in Managing and Preserving Electronic Records*

In 2002, the General Accounting Office (GAO) conducted a review of NARA's ERA program. The excerpts below from the GAO report indicate some of the challenges to successful execution that were identified at that time.

In response to the challenges associated with managing and preserving electronic records, NARA has performed an assessment of governmentwide records management—an important first step that identified several problems, including the inadequacy of guidance on electronic records, the low priority generally given to records management, and the lack of technology tools to manage electronic records. While NARA has plans to improve its guidance and address the need for technology, it has not yet formulated a strategy to deal with the stature of records management programs across government. Further, it has no strategy for acquiring the kind of comprehensive information on records management that would be provided by systematic inspections and evaluations of federal records programs. Without such a strategy, records management will likely continue to be considered a low-priority "support" activity lacking appropriate management attention, and NARA will not acquire information needed to address problems in agency records management and guidance. Inadequacies in records management put at risk records that may be valuable: records providing information on essential government functions, information that is necessary to protect government and citizen interests, and information that is significant for the historical record.

NARA's effort to acquire an advanced electronic records archive is at risk. NARA is not meeting its schedule for the ERA system, largely because of flaws in how the schedule was developed. As a result, the schedule will be compressed, leaving less time for completing essential planning tasks. In addition, NARA has not yet improved IT management capabilities that would reduce the risks inherent in its effort to acquire ERA. Without these capabilities, NARA risks spending funds to acquire a system that does not meet mission needs and requirements, effectively work with existing systems, or provide adequate security over the information it contains.[1]

---

[1] General Accounting Office (GAO). 2002. *Information Management: Challenges in Managing and Preserving Electronic Records*, report number GAO-02-586. GAO, Washington, D.C., pp. 32-33.

C

Briefers to the Study Committee

Although the briefers listed below provided many useful inputs to the committee, they were not asked to endorse the conclusions or recommendations, nor did they see the final draft of the report before its release.

AUGUST 8-9, 2002
WASHINGTON, D.C.

John Carlin, Archivist of the United States
Kenneth Thibodeau, Director, Electronic Records Archives Program, NARA
Robert Chadduck, Research Director, Electronic Records Archives Program, NARA
Reagan Moore, San Diego Supercomputer Center
Michael Lesk, National Science Foundation

NOVEMBER 5-6, 2002
WASHINGTON, D.C.

James Ostell, Chief, Information Engineering Branch, National Center for Biotechnology Information
Anne Van Camp, Research Libraries Group
Michael Miller, Archivist, Federal Bureau of Investigation
James Gray, Microsoft Research
Anna K. Nelson, American University
Joseph King, National Space Science Data Center
James Olson, Sabbath, Inc.

FEBRUARY 27-28, 2003
WASHINGTON, D.C.

Laura Campbell, Associate Librarian for Strategic Initiatives and Chief Information Officer, Library of Congress
Rick Barry, Principal, Barry Associates
MacKenzie Smith, Massachusetts Institute of Technology Libraries
Robert Chadduck, Research Director, Electronic Records Archives Program, NARA

What Is CSTB?

The Computer Science and Telecommunications Board (CSTB) was established in 1986 as a part of the National Research Council to provide independent advice to the nation on technical and public policy issues relating to computing and communications. Composed of leaders from industry and academia, CSTB conducts studies of critical national issues and makes recommendations to government, industry, and academia. CSTB also provides a neutral meeting ground for consideration of complex issues where resolution and action may be premature. It convenes discussions that bring together principals from the public and private sectors, assuring consideration of key perspectives. The majority of CSTB's work is requested by federal agencies and Congress, consistent with its National Academies context.

A pioneer in framing and analyzing Internet policy issues, CSTB is unique in its comprehensive scope and effective, interdisciplinary appraisal of technical, economic, social, and policy issues. Cybersecurity, critical infrastructure protection, and the trustworthiness of information systems have been cross-cutting themes in CSTB's work. Several of its reports have become classics in the field, and CSTB continues to address these topics as they grow in importance. Its program on information technology and society has explored such topics as nationwide identity systems and the use of the Internet under crisis conditions. CSTB has also assessed and recommended enhanced IT strategies for a number of agencies of the federal government.

To do its work, CSTB draws on some of the best minds in the country and from around the world, inviting experts to participate in its projects as a public service. Studies are conducted by balanced committees whose members have no direct financial interests in the topics they are addressing. Those committees meet, confer electronically, and build analyses through their deliberations. Additional expertise is tapped in a rigorous process of review and critique, further enhancing the quality of CSTB reports. By engaging groups of principals, CSTB gets the facts and insights critical to assessing key issues.

The mission of CSTB is to

- *Respond to requests* from the government, nonprofit organizations, and private industry for advice on computer and telecommunications issues and from the government for advice on computer and telecommunications systems planning, utilization, and modernization;
- *Monitor and promote the health* of computer science and telecommunications, with attention to issues of human resources, information infrastructure, and societal impacts;
- *Initiate and conduct studies* that treat computer science, technology, and telecommunications as critical resources; and
- *Foster interaction* among the disciplines underlying computing and telecommunications technologies and other fields, at large and within the National Academies.

CSTB projects address a diverse range of topics affected by the evolution of information technology. Completed reports include *Beyond Productivity: Information Technology, Innovation, and Creativity*; *Who Goes There? Authentication Through the Lens of Privacy*; *Information Technology for Counterterrorism: Immediate Actions and Future Possibilities*; *Cybersecurity Today and Tomorrow: Pay Now or Pay Later*; *Youth, Pornography, and the Internet*; *Broadband: Bringing Home the Bits*; *LC21: A Digital Strategy for the Library of Congress*; and *The Digital Dilemma: Intellectual Property in the Information Age*. For further information about CSTB reports and active projects, see <http://cstb.org>.